UNIVERSAL OR SELECTIVE? THE DEBATE ON REFORMING INCOME SECURITY IN CANADA

Universal or Selective?

Policy
Study
Series

Ontario
Economic
Council

the debate on reforming
income security in Canada

Michael Mendelson

ISSN 0227-0005
ISBN 0-7743-6230-8

Michael Mendelson is a research officer with the Ontario Economic Council.

This report reflects the views of the author and not necessarily those of the Ontario Economic Council or the Government of Ontario. The Council establishes policy questions to be investigated and commissions research projects, but it does not influence the conclusions or recommendations of authors. The decision to sponsor publication of this study was based on its competence and relevance to public policy and was made with the advice of anonymous referees expert in the area.

Contents

Acknowledgments

I would like to thank Charles Kahn for his assistance in organizing this report and identifying many key questions. I have also benefited from a comprehensive set of comments from Jonathan Kesselman. These were particularly helpful since much of my approach to income security has been shaped by Kesselman's work on the universality–selectivity issue. Another important source of inspiration has been research done at the Economic Council of Canada, especially by J. Eden Cloutier. Although I criticize Cloutier's conclusions, this by no means diminishes the importance of his contribution.

This report could not have been written without the support of the Ontario Economic Council. The Council has provided a stimulating environment for independent research, free of any constraint except those of relevance to policy and scholarly quality. My colleagues at the Ontario Economic Council have given me much assistance with comments and suggestions on successive drafts. I would like in particular to thank Enid Slack, Tassos Belessiotis, Lorie Tarshis, Doug Crocker, and Derek Jones. Freya Godard's editing has added substantially to the clarity of the study. The Council has also provided a cheerful and exceptionally competent librarian, Ann Chin, who has invariably produced texts to match my often vague requests. Nancy Cole and Nancy Savoie have typed several drafts of this report. Their patience with my numerous revisions has been remarkable. Their accuracy and promptness have helped to create a much better product than would have otherwise been possible.

Finally, I would like to thank my wife, Marsha Cohen. I am certain I would never have completed this project without her unfailing encouragement and constant support.

I, alone, of course, remain responsible for any errors, omissions, or misinterpretations that remain.

UNIVERSAL OR SELECTIVE? THE DEBATE ON REFORMING INCOME SECURITY IN CANADA

1
Concepts and definitions

INTRODUCTION

Income security programs that pay only to those with low incomes are usually called 'selective,' while programs that pay regardless of income are called 'universal.' Since well before World War II there has been continuing debate over whether income security programs should be universal or selective. In the earliest days of the income security system, virtually all programs were selective. Following the Beveridge report (1942), universality became the favoured approach. But today in Canada, the pendulum of mainstream opinion has swung back. Many Canadians apparently believe that the desirability of greater selectivity is now self-evident and that only questions of implementation remain.[1] This report argues to the contrary, that is, that much of the present support for selectivity is not well founded.

The first problem is to define more precisely the words 'universal' and 'selective.' Anything from a program in which everyone receives a payment to a program in which anyone may be paid *if* he or she meets eligibility criteria has been described as universal. Here the term is used in a more restricted sense. By 'universal' it is meant that the gross amount paid (before taxes) does not decrease as the income or wealth of the recipient increases. The term 'selective' will be used here to mean the opposite of universal. A selective program is one in which the gross amount paid *is* adjusted according to the income or wealth of the recipient. Thus every program is either universal or selective.

1 For example, the President of the Treasury Board reported to a gathering of business executives that 'the government is examining the obvious shortcomings of the universality concept in social welfare programs, with a view to finding a better approach' (as paraphrased in *The Public Sector*, 11 August 1980).

While these definitions are the same as those used by other researchers (for example, Garfinkel 1981b), many Canadians would not consider both Family Allowance and Unemployment Insurance universal. This difficulty may be avoided by further dividing universal programs into two groups: demogrants and social insurance. Demogrants pay the same amount to everyone in a broadly defined demographic group such as the aged. This paper will use the term social insurance programs to refer to those that maintain earmarked contributions and in which the amount paid is related to the contributions, although those may not be the sole source of financing. This interpretation of social insurance is similar to the one adopted by the Canadian judicial system.

Another problem for any study of the income security system is to define some reasonable limits, for there is a continuously changing set of income security programs that make payments, known as transfers, to individuals or families. Such programs can come in all shapes and sizes, and they have no precise, accepted definition. It is particularly difficult to draw a line between income security and the tax system. For example, the Refundable Child Tax Credit (RCTC) in 1979 paid each family up to $200 per child. But even families entitled to a payment may not have received a cheque if their income tax was more than the RCTC. The benefit may instead have been in the form of a reduction in the tax payable. A rational person could hardly care about this distinction: whether a cheque was sent or the tax was reduced, the result remained of equal value. But there is also an income tax exemption for each child. Since the RCTC is usually regarded as an income security program, does this mean that the income tax exemption is also an income security program?

One difference between the RCTC and the tax exemption is that the former is of benefit to those who pay no tax, since the RCTC is payable even if no tax is owed. It may be more than a reduction in tax liability and is therefore called 'refundable.' The income tax exemption, on the other hand, is only of benefit if tax is otherwise due. In this study programs that provide refundable payments to individuals are regarded as income security programs. This is essentially an arbitrary distinction, for a reduction in tax is as valuable to those who receive it as a direct payment, and a decrease in transfers costs as much to those who bear it as a tax increase of equal amount. Although this paper is primarily about income security programs, they will usually be discussed in the context of the tax–transfer system as a whole.

Even with this restricted definition, income security in Canada was a $20 billion business in 1979. With total disposable income at $172 billion (Statistics Canada, *Systems of Accounts: National Income and Expenditure Accounts*) it was the source of 12 per cent of Canadian incomes. Table 1 lists expendi-

TABLE 1
Expenditures on income security programs ($000,000)

	1977		1978		1979	
	$	%	$	%	$	%
Demogrants						
Family and Youth Allowance	2084	13	2224	12	1695	8
Old Age Security	3519	21	3933	21	4571	23
Demogrants sub-total	5603	34	6157	33	6266	31
Social Insurance						
Canada and Quebec Pension	1356	8	1701	9	2089	10
Unemployment Insurance	3904	24	4536	24	4040	20
Workers' Compensation	900	5	1080	6	1223	6
Veterans' benefits*	601	4	646	3	702	3
Insurance sub-total	6761	41	7963	43	8054	40
Universal programs, total	12364	75	14120	76	14320	71
Selective programs						
Guaranteed Income Sup.	1079	7	1206	6	1402	7
Spouse's Allowance	94	1	105	1	122	1
Refundable Child Credit	–	–	–	–	810	4
Provincial tax credits (est.)	700	4	750	4	800	4
Social Assistance	2274	14	2456	13	2744	14
Selective sub-total	4147	25	4517	24	5878	29
Total, all programs	16511	100	18637	100	20198	100

SOURCE: Statistics Canada, *Social Security*, *National Programs* and *Government Finance in Accordance with the System of National Accounts* for 1977 and 1978 figures. 1979 preliminary estimates provided by Statistics Canada. Estimates for the Old Age Security and Guaranteed Supplement and Spouse's Allowance are derived by assuming that each program has the same share of the total of the three programs as was the case in 1976 (75%, 23%, and 2% respectively). Estimate for the Refundable Child Tax Credit is from Canada (1979). Estimates of provincial tax credits are only a very rough projection to keep totals realistic. Provincial tax credits were $690 million in 1976 (Statistics Canada, *Consolidated Government Finance: Fiscal Year Ended Nearest to December 31*).
* Veterans' benefits are a mixture of social insurance and selective transfers. Many of the provincial tax credits are also not selective.

tures in each type of program in 1977, 1978, and 1979. It also analyses these figures according to their percentage of total expenditures on income security. In all three years the largest expenditures were made through social insurance programs, with demogrants second. Outlays on selective programs were somewhat less than the total for demogrants. A slight change towards selective programs was brought about by the introduction of the RCTC and a reduction in Family Allowance and Unemployment Insurance. A trend for old-age programs to increase may also be seen, largely because of the maturing of the Canada and Quebec Pension Plans and the aging of the population.

In Canada, proposals for greater selectivity have been made for both demogrants and social insurance programs. Family Allowance, which pays a flat amount for each child in a family regardless of income (subject to some provincial variations), has been a prime target for reform. In 1979 it was reduced by approximately 20 per cent to provide funds for the RCTC, and so has already partially been converted to a selective program. Groups as diverse as the Economic Council of Canada (ECC 1978) and the Canadian Council on Social Development (CCSD 1979) have called for still more selectivity. Similarly, Unemployment Insurance (UI) has been a favourite target among social insurance programs. While proposals for UI have generally been for measures such as family income surcharges (Osberg 1979), which are not directly selective, such policies have the same objective as the proposals for greater selectivity.

These and similar proposals are the basis of the universality–selectivity debate. This study is a 'road map' to that debate. It does not present new empirical or conceptual material; instead it attempts, using the most up-to-date and, wherever possible, Canadian sources, to draw together many of the disparate contributions that have already been made to the debate. Its aim is to help the interested reader make a well-informed judgment on the policies advocated by each side of the universality–selectivity debate.

Economists usually use two criteria for judging policy issues: equity and efficiency. 'Equity' is another word for 'fairness.' 'Efficiency' in the most general sense means a situation in which the aggregate level of well-being, or the value of consumption, is as high as possible. In the following two chapters the universality–selectivity debate is viewed from the perspective of each of these criteria in turn. Chapter 2, on equity, analyses the effect of various policies on the distribution of income, how that can be measured, and the objectives of income security programs in redistributing income. Chapter 3 discusses the main aspects of efficiency with respect to income security: the effects on work effort, on savings, and on administration.

Non-economic perspectives may be as important as, or even more important than, economic considerations in the universality–selectivity debate. Chapter 4 reviews some crucial social and institutional factors. This includes the question of 'stigma' as well as the effect on federalism of changing the structure of our income security system. In the fifth chapter, policy proposals for greater selectivity are reviewed in light of the analysis in the preceding chapters. The last chapter is a brief summary of the arguments and their implications for the design of a model income security system.

Although this study attempts to be comprehensive, the universality–selectivity debate touches on almost every important issue in the area of income security programs, and on occasion, therefore, a point is only mentioned and not analysed. Inevitably, some points will have been missed entirely. Each chapter begins with a summary of the contents, which the reader may use as a guide to finding sections of special interest.

Before discussing the effects of restructuring Canada's income security system, however, there is a question of what programs to compare: a very poorly designed universal program may be worse than a well-thought-out selective program, but this does not tell us much about the comparative attractiveness of universality or selectivity in general. This problem is often solved by comparing programs that entail equal expenditure by governments. This method of analysis as applied to income security programs is presented in the next section and is the method used throughout the remaining chapters.

COMPARING PROGRAMS

There is an infinite range of alternatives to any public policy; some would result in greater government spending, others in less. When seeking substitutes for present policies, we often wish to know whether it is possible to do better with the existing resources. For this reason an approach often adopted is to look only at alternatives that would require equal government spending. This is known as 'differential' analysis.

Most government expenditures are on goods and services, and differential analysis seems appropriate for these programs. But if transfers are also seen as expenditures, this method is not suitable for comparing income security programs. For example, a tax exemption could be replaced by an income security program designed exactly so that there would be no change in either the effects on individuals or on government spending for goods and services. Ordinarily therefore, the substitution of income transfers for identical tax exemptions would be seen as merely cosmetic. But if transfers are defined as government expenditures and tax exemptions are a decrease in revenue, there would be a great increase in expenditures and an equal increase in revenue. According to a differential approach, these alternatives would not even be comparable; yet they are really identical.

Furthermore, many proposals for greater selectivity would entail a reduction in total transfer payments rather than the same amount being spent differently. For example, it is often argued that the effect of family allowances on the poor could be the same for, say, $1 billion and that government expenditures could then be reduced by the remaining $700 million. This alternative cannot be analysed by the differential approach if transfers are regarded as government expenditure.

A method of analysis that does not impose arbitrary limits on reductions in tax compared to increases in transfers is to treat transfers as negative taxes. If, then, one of the options under consideration requires an increase in transfers, it is compensated for by an equal increase in taxes, so that there is no change in government spending on goods and services (or government deficits). Similarly, a decrease in transfers must be distributed through a decrease in taxes just sufficient to offset the change. For example, reducing the Family Allowance to $1 billion with a $700 million decrease in spending would be compensated for by a $700 million reduction in taxes. This is the standard and well-accepted way of comparing tax–transfer programs in economic studies. [2]

For some, it may seem unusual to say that government spending does not change when transfers increase. The point, of course, is that government spending on *goods and services* remains unchanged. More transfers may flow through government, but once these transfers are paid to individuals they remain part of the non-government sector. In an accounting sense, public expenditures will rise as transfers rise even if the change is exactly compensated for by an increase in taxes. But in an economic sense there has been no increase in resources devoted to public use, only a redistribution among individuals. What is relevant economically is the changes in people's behaviour that may result from shifts in incentives. These are not related to the level of transfers and cannot be measured by the flow of transfers through government. These questions are discussed further in the following chapters. For now the point is only that for transfer programs differential analysis does not have to deal with the macro-economic implications of different sizes of the public sector. Public spending on goods and services remains fixed.

A serious problem is that one must describe how additional revenue might be raised and how tax decreases might be distributed. Obviously, if there is a

---

2 See Break (1974), Musgrave and Musgrave (1976), and Fallis (1980) for a review of the methods discussed here. Break recommends differential analysis for transfer policy comparisons, noting that 'this represents a special case of differential tax incidence' because alternative policies are 'simply a combination of positive and negative taxes (or negative and positive transfers)' (Break 1974, 129).

reduction in taxes of $700 milion, it might be distributed in a number of ways: an increase in the income tax exemption, a decrease in tobacco taxes, or even an increase in the Child Tax Credit to name just three possibilities. How do we decide which tax reduction to adopt for our calculations? Similarly if there is a tax increase it may be collected in any one way, or combination of ways. How can one tax collection method be selected?

In this study it is assumed, unless otherwise stated, that any tax increases or decreases would be distributed so as not to change the percentage tax contribution of each income group to total tax revenue. Thus, for example, if the 20 per cent of the population with the highest income paid 50 per cent of total tax revenue, then given a $1 billion reduction in taxes, this group would get 50 per cent, or $500 million, of the tax decrease.[3] This assumption may not be too unrealistic in Canada, at least in so far as revenue is raised through the income tax. Tax reductions have been made largely by increasing income tax exemptions, particularly through indexation for inflation, which preserves relative tax shares. Furthermore, the evidence seems to suggest that tax shares (counting all taxes) have remained stable (see, for example, Gillespie 1978). This assumption is also implicit in recent Canadian empirical research on the distributive effects of the tax-transfer system (Cloutier 1978).

Since this study uses the differential approach, it will be assumed in discussing any policy that requires changes in government revenue, that there is a compensating tax change, unless otherwise mentioned. This allows a comparison between various policy proposals. In the next chapter's review of the distributional effects of different universal and selective programs, the distribution of tax reductions will be included. In Canada, tax changes resulting from income security policies have been largely ignored. In the third chapter, the discussion of incentives will also include the effects of tax changes, whereas only transfer changes have usually been taken into account.

3 This implies that any change in revenue will increase or decrease every income group's marginal tax rates in proportion to the change in revenue, before consideration of the marginal tax rates associated with the benefits of the program being financed.

2

The distribution of income

It has ordinarily been assumed that increasing the selectivity of transfer payments would entail a redistribution of income only to those with low incomes. In the first part of this chapter it is argued that this assumption is incorrect and that increased selectivity may instead help both the poor and the rich at the expense of middle-income groups. Describing distribution simply as the average benefit for each income group is also problematic. Among the factors not taken into account are adjustment for family size, distribution of income within groups, and a lifetime concept of income. As is shown in the second part of this chapter, these factors will alter the view of the distributive consequences of income security programs.

Much of the discussion of effects on income distribution is confined to the first round or immediate impact of a policy. In the longer run, behavioural changes and shifting of taxes will distort this immediate impact. Whether this should be a prime consideration in designing programs is the subject of the third section of this chapter.

Increasing the income of persons with low incomes may not be the only purpose for income security programs. They may also be required for other distributive objectives – such as ensuring fair treatment of families with similar incomes but differing needs. Finally, there are a number of non-distributive objectives to which income security programs may be addressed. One example is the optimal allocation of income over the lifetime. Other objectives are discussed in the final section of this chapter.

THE NET BENEFIT OF INCOME SECURITY PROGRAMS

In the daily media, the benefits of government programs are often described simply as the goods, services, or money distributed. For example, the benefits of family allowance are said to be $20 a month per child. But government programs are, unfortunately, not costless; they have a price tag although it may be hidden. What is usually described as the benefit of an income security program is not the 'benefit' as it would ordinarily be understood, that is, the *gain* in the income of those affected by the program. Instead, it is simply the amount of money paid out. To find someone's gain (or loss) in income, the amount paid for a program has to be subtracted from the amount received from the program. The difference is the *net* benefit. To discuss transfers paid from income security programs without calculation of net benefits is to perpetuate the illusion that government programs are costless.

Clearly there are many different ways that net benefits could be calculated. This is because taxes are not earmarked for use in specific programs and there is no way of saying which taxes have gone for what. For example, we know that $1.7 billion was spent through the Family Allowance program, but we do not know which taxes financed it or how much was financed by taxes as opposed to borrowing, and we do not know who would bear the cost of these taxes or ultimately of the borrowing. If we ask, 'How was a program financed?', there can be no definitive reply; in fact it may not be a very sensible question.

On the other hand, the question 'what would the tax reductions be if this program were cancelled?' has a reasonable answer. This is just the analysis discussed in Chapter 1, in which one of the alternatives is no program at all, so that the total cost is used to reduce taxes. To find the net benefit for an individual, we need to find what his or her tax reduction would be if there were no program. This may be described as the incremental tax burden as a result of the program. Subtracting the incremental tax burden from the transfer paid gives an estimate of net benefit. Of course, as discussed above, a tax reduction can be distributed in a number of ways. In this paper it is assumed that tax changes are distributed to maintain the existing tax shares of income groups. The reader should note that other assumptions are possible.

A program such as Family Allowance may be used to illustrate these concepts. Say Mr and Mrs Middle-Income have one child under eighteen and receive a transfer payment of $240 a year from Family Allowance. But the Family Allowance is taxable income. If the Middle-Incomes' tax on the $240 is $50, then the *net transfer* is $190. This is where the popular writing usually stops. But the government could lower taxes were it not for the Middle-Incomes' $190 and all the other net transfers. Say that the family's tax bill is $150 higher than it would be if there were no Family Allowance program. Then the *net benefit* to the Middle-Incomes is $40: this is the change in their income as a result of the program.

What this means for the universality–selectivity debate is that, while universal programs may pay transfers that do not increase as income decreases, the *net* benefits of universal programs may increase as income falls. If the tax system is progressive, the net benefits of a universal program will also be progressive.[4] In fact, the net benefits of universal programs will be progressive even if the tax system is neutral or mildly regressive. A universal program may indeed pay money to those who do not need it, but this does not mean that it delivers net benefits to them. Many wealthy persons who receive a universal transfer payment in fact have a net loss rather than a net benefit, because their taxes would be lower without the program than their benefits with the program.

An empirical analysis of distribution of transfers and some costs of income security programs is contained in Cloutier (1978). Cloutier's findings are presented in Table 2, where the direct costs and benefits of income transfer programs for each income quintile are estimated. Income quintiles are derived by ordering all families and individuals according to the size of their income and then dividing the population into five groups. Thus the 20 per cent of families and individuals with the lowest income are in the first quintile, while the 20 per cent with the highest income are in the fifth quintile. Cloutier's findings will be discussed further below in the context of ways to measure the consequences for income distribution, but it seems evident from them that there is not necessarily a great difference in the distribution of net benefits between selective and universal programs. For example there is not much difference in the net benefits of the demogrant Old Age Security and the selective Guaranteed Income Supplement.

---

4 In the context of the tax system, 'progressive' means that those who have more income pay a greater proportion of their income in taxes. There is no widely accepted meaning for 'progressive' in the context of a transfer program. This paper will say that net benefits are progressively distributed when the amount of the net benefit increases as income decreases. A regressive tax system is one in which the poor pay a greater proportion of their income than the wealthy. A regressive transfer system is here defined as one in which net benefits are greater for the wealthy than the poor. Notice that with this definition, the net benefits of a regressive transfer program might be a greater proportion of income for the poor than the rich, so that the definitions are not symmetrical for taxes and transfers. Often the term 'progressive' has been used to be precisely symmetrical in the tax and transfer system (Wolfson 1980a). The definition in this paper seems more in keeping with common usage, although not necessarily with usage in the academic literature. A program that gave $100,000 to those with a million dollar income and $2000 to those with $10,000 income would not commonly be considered 'progressive.'

TABLE 2
Distribution of benefits and contributions in social security programs for 1975 (percentages)

Family after-tax income quintile	Family Allowance		Unemployment Insurance		Old Age Security		Guaranteed Income Supplement		Canada and Quebec Pension Plans	
	benefit	contrib.	benefit	contrib.	benefit	contrib.	benefit	contrib.	benefit	contrib.
First	5.7	0.1	8.1	2.1	38.0	0.2	47.4	0.2	26.8	2.4
Second	12.6	5.1	22.0	11.4	31.3	6.2	33.1	4.8	30.8	13.6
Third	21.9	17.0	25.0	20.8	13.6	15.5	7.1	13.9	18.4	21.6
Fourth	27.6	27.6	22.6	27.0	8.2	24.3	5.6	24.8	12.7	27.2
Fifth	32.2	50.2	22.3	38.7	8.9	53.8	6.8	56.3	11.3	35.2

SOURCE: J.E. Cloutier (1978)

Cloutier's findings are, however, based only on the income tax, taxes that may be paid on the transfer itself, and earmarked contributions (Cloutier calls these 'direct' taxes). If the share of other taxes had been included as well, the percentage shares of contributions would appear less progressive; therefore the distribution of net benefits would also appear less progressive. Of course, it should be noted that contribution shares are not a percentage of each quintiles' income; rather they are the percentage of total program financing contributed by each quintile. If the fifth quintile has 40 per cent of total income, in a strictly proportionate tax system their percentage contribution would be 40 per cent. Thus the tax system upon which Cloutier's findings are based is not very progressive. Even if the tax system were less progressive it appears that the wealthiest income groups would still be net losers from income transfer programs, whether universal or selective.

To summarize: the most serious problem in much of the popular writing on selectivity is that it ignores the effects of tax savings and transfer reductions, treating both as wealth that somehow goes nowhere and comes from nobody (for example, Simon 1979, Crispo 1979). The benefits of various transfer programs cannot be judged in isolation from the taxes associated with each program. The first step in analysing the effects of increased selectivity is therefore to look at the net benefit of the tax–transfer package. The net benefit is the transfer minus the incremental tax borne as a result of the transfer program. For some the net benefit will be positive, and for others it will be negative. The sum of net benefits will be zero. It is the distribution of net benefits, and not the distribution of transfers, that represents 'the bottom line.' The distribution of net benefits for *both* universal and selective programs will be progressive so long as the tax system is progressive, or at least not very regressive.

THE DISTRIBUTIVE EFFECTS OF INCREASED SELECTIVITY

If the distributive effects of a transfer program are its net benefits, then the distributive effects of a change in programs is the change in net benefits. This appears to be a simple logical deduction, but it is a step that even many of the more careful studies fail to make. Yet it is an elementary principle of public finance that 'in determining the distributional changes that result from an adjustment in budget policy, we must trace both losses and gains that may occur to particular individuals' (Musgrave 1959, 229).

One of the most influential Canadian arguments for greater selectivity is in the Economic Council of Canada's fifteenth Annual Review, *A Time For Reason* (1978). From Cloutier's findings, the ECC points out that Family

Allowance is 'the least progressive of the five social security schemes examined here.' On this basis they conclude that the 'recently announced reductions in the family allowance payments coupled with the introduction of income related supplements' (the Refundable Child Tax Credit) ... 'could have gone further' (ECC 1978, 112). On the same grounds of increased progressivity the Canadian Council on Social Development recommends 'completely recovering family allowance and old age payments from recipients with incomes above average family income' (CCSD 1979, 10).[5]

Neither the ECC nor the CCSD estimates the *change* in net benefits that would result from their recommendations. The question is not simply whether the new net benefits are more progressive than the old; rather the question is how are the new net benefits *minus* the old distributed? Although both the ECC and the CCSD suggest that government savings may be used to enrich anti-poverty programs, neither sees this as a necessary pre-condition to ensure that their recommendations lead to a desirable redistribution of income. But a reduction and rechannelling of transfers can have surprising consequences for the redistribution of income: it is not obvious that the outcomes would always be those favoured by the CCSD and the ECC.

Moving to greater selectivity may mean that both the poor and the wealthy will be net winners, the former from increased transfers and the latter from decreased taxes, while the middle-income group will be net losers. To demonstrate how this could happen, Table 3 illustrates the effect of moving from a hypothetical universal Program A to a hypothetical selective Program B. Imagine that there are eight million families in the country and that Program A distributes $3000 to each as a flat non-categorical demogrant. Then the total budget required for the program is $24 billion. Each income quintile bears a percentage share of the tax burden, with the lowest quintile paying 1 per cent of the costs and the highest quintile paying 51 per cent. This approximates an estimate of the 'direct' tax burden in Canada's social security system in 1975 (Cloutier 1978, 27).

One can then calculate the average tax burden per family in each quintile, that is, the average increment in tax for each family in each quintile because of this program. This is simply equal to the total share of the tax burden for that quintile divided by the number of families. Subtracting the tax burden from the positive transfer of $3000 gives the average net benefit in the

---

5 The CCSD is not clear whether 'recovering' means decreasing the transfer paid or collecting after the payment has been made. In the latter case, this is not strictly a recommendation for increased selectivity as it has been defined in this paper. Nevertheless, the distributive effects discussed here still apply.

TABLE 3
Illustration of potential winners and losers in moving to greater selectivity

Quintile	No. of families[a] (000,000)	Share of financing[b] %	Program A			Program B			Net income change, B − A $
			Transfer per family $	Tax per family $	Net benefit $	Transfer per family $	Tax per family $	Net benefit $	
1	1.6	1	3000	−150	2850	6000	−90	−5910	3060
2	1.6	7	3000	−1050	1950	3000	−630	2370	420
3	1.6	16	3000	−2400	600	0	−1440	−1440	−2040
4	1.6	25	3000	−3750	−750	0	−2250	−2250	−1500
5	1.6	51	3000	−7650	−4650	0	−4590	−4590	60
Total	8	100	24 billion	24 billion		14.4 billion	14.4 billion		0

a Approximate number of economic families (related persons sharing a common dwelling unit) plus the number of unattached individuals. Statistics Canada (1975)

b From Cloutier (1978). Shares of direct financing for Canada's social security system in 1975, rounded for easier calculation. Does not necessarily portray how a real program of family demogrants would be financed.

income class. The net benefit in this example is progressive because of the tax system, as illustrated in the sixth column of Table 3.

In the search for a more equitable distribution of income, and lower taxes, it might be suggested that we could save money and at the same time give more to the poor by replacing Program A with a more selective Program B. Program B would pay an average of $6000 to those in the first income quintile and an average of $3000 to those in the second quintile. The poor would get more because of the higher transfer payments, and the program would cost substantially less – in this illustration 40 per cent less. However not only the changes in transfers but also taxes have to be counted. Because the middle-income groups lose their transfers and get relatively less tax relief, they are the big net losers in the move from A to B. On the other hand, the upper-income groups gain from the tax relief and are somewhat better off than with Program A.

Column B−A records the net benefits under B less the net benefits under A and thus tells us who gains and who loses from substituting Program B for Program A. Column B−A is identical to the change in transfer payment plus tax saving distributed across income groups using the differential method so that government spending on goods and services remains constant. As we can see in this illustration, the poor are substantially better off with a gain of over $3000 for the lowest income quintile. The second quintile is a little better off with a gain of $420. The fifth quintile, the wealthiest, is also a little better off with an average gain of $60. But the middle and upper-middle group are the big losers: there is an average loss per family of $2040 and $1500 for the third and fourth quintiles respectively.

While Table 3 is merely an illustration, it demonstrates that progressive income redistribution does not necessarily follow from converting universal programs into selective programs. Assessment of income distribution effects requires estimation of the change in net benefits. Otherwise poor Mr and Mrs Middle-Income, who no doubt rely on the advice of journalists and research institutes, may find themselves unwittingly bearing the entire burden of improved benefits to the poor and a little tax relief for the wealthy.

Of course, this implies that a decrease in transfer payments is just the same as an increase in taxes. This is correct so long as we are concerned only about net incomes. A rational individual should not care whether taxes are increased by $100 or transfers decreased by $100: either way there is $100 less income (Kesselman and Garfinkel 1978, 183). However, one difference is the amount of money flowing through government and therefore the size of government budgets.

Government budgets, as traditionally recorded, will be larger with a transfer increase than a comparable tax decrease. With the publication of a tax expenditure budget in the United States for the last several years, and the publication of a similar tax expenditure budget in Canada, (Canada 1979), there is now a growing awareness that these differences are merely a question of the accounting system and have little to do with the actual size of government. As discussed in Chapter 1, government expenditures on goods and services are an appropriation of resources that might have otherwise been available for non-government use. But government expenditures on transfer payments redistribute the ability to appropriate goods and services between individuals. They do not represent government use of resources. Combining transfer expenditures with spending on goods and services creates a false impression of the size and growth of government.

This can be illustrated by a family dedicated to sharing its income, where decisions as to income sharing are made by a non-earning father. Say the mother earns $20,000, the daughter $18,000, and the son $10,000. Each gives the father half of his or her income (a tax), which he then divides equally among all four family members including himself (a transfer). The father therefore collects $24,000 and keeps $6000 for himself. Is his expenditure $24,000? If the father took all of everyone's income and then redistributed it equally among the three earners but kept nothing for himself, would his expenditure now be $48,000 or nothing? Obviously it is nonsense to add into the father's expenditure money that he gives to others. It is equally nonsense to add transfers to total government expenditures. The size of government budgets, so far as they are affected by a preference for transfers over comparable tax decreases, is only an accounting consideration and should have no effect on the universality versus selectivity debate.[6]

It has been argued above that changes in income security programs have to be analysed in terms of changes in net benefits. The net benefits for both the poor and the wealthy may be improved by an increase in selectivity; those with middle incomes may be made worse off. But there are also many problems in measuring the income distribution of Canadian families and individuals simply by ordering them according to their current income. For example, most of those in the first quintile will be single individuals while

6 A more rational budget would include transfers in the revenue side. A budget might then consist of spending on goods and services on the expenditure side and revenue from the 'normal tax schedule' less tax expenditures and transfers on the revenue side. Until this happens admonitions to ignore the effect of transfers on the size of government will have little effect. See Mendelson (1981).

some in the second and third quintile will be large families. Can we assume that individuals in the first quintile are in greater need of transfer payments than families in the second, as is implicit in the ECC argument?

MEASURING INCOME DISTRIBUTION

Adjustment for family size
Table 4 shows the distribution of families and individuals within the income quintiles in 1975. As can be seen, individuals and childless couples make up 81.8 per cent and 63.5 per cent of the total in the first and second income quintiles respectively, but are only 48.6 per cent of the population as a whole. It is thus hardly surprising that less Family Allowances went to the first two income quintiles. Furthermore, it is quite possible that a family in the third quintile will be worse off than an individual in the second quintile. To adjust for family size we require an index of the relative needs of families of various sizes. For illustration, Table 5 is an index based on 1975 Statistics Canada low income cut-offs for cities with greater than 500,000 population (Statistics Canada 1975).

Family incomes can be divided by these indices to arrive at adjusted income that could then be used to re-arrange families into income quintiles. The flow of transfers, such as family allowance, into these new quintiles would give a better idea of whether transfers are going to those in need. It is evident that the distribution for many programs will be very different after adjustment for family size. This is substantiated in an empirical study by Morgan (1980).

Another way of taking account of family size would be to estimate net income flows above and below a defined poverty line adjusted for family size. For example, the Statistics Canada low-income cut-offs were used for this purpose in Smith et al. (1979). We would then look at the net income change resulting from the new policy for families above and below the poverty lines. This would still require calculating the net benefits for each policy and subtracting the new from the old. This method has the disadvantage of not showing any redistribution among families below the line or among those above the line; instead it divides the whole population into two groups. This does not allow a very fine measure of the distributive effects on society, and we could not tell which of the middle- or upper-income groups were bearing an additional burden.

Unfortunately Smith et al. do not calculate the net benefits of the existing programs, let alone the net income change resulting from a recommended policy. They focus instead on the flow of transfers without discussion of

TABLE 4
Percentage distribution of families and individuals within income quintiles, Canada 1975

| | Quintiles | | | | | |
	1	2	3	4	5	Total
Family size						
Unattached individuals	69.5	38.4	20.9	8.8	2.5	28.0
Married couples only	12.3	25.1	22.7	23.2	19.8	20.6
Married couples, one child	7.9	23.0	45.6	58.7	67.6	40.5
Married couples, children, and/or other relatives	0.3	1.4	2.5	3.9	6.5	2.9
All other families	10.0	12.1	8.3	5.3	3.6	7.9
Other characteristics						
Age of head 65+	40.8	25.0	10.0	4.9	4.4	17.0
Male head	47.3	68.9	85.4	93.8	97.7	78.6
Female head	52.7	31.1	14.6	6.2	2.3	21.4

SOURCE: Statistics Canada (1975)

TABLE 5
Index of needs based on family size

Family size:	1	2	3	4	5	6	7+
Low income cut-off:	$3829	$5549	$7081	$8422	$9414	$10,335	$11,333
Index for family size:	1	1.45	1.85	2.20	2.46	2.70	2.96

SOURCE: Statistics Canada (1975)

costs. They conclude that '*Almost 90 per cent of unemployment insurance benefits paid in 1975, then, were received by family units with incomes in excess of the low income thresholds*' (Smith et al. 1979, 29, emphasis in original). But if over 90 per cent of the *costs* were also paid by families with income over the thresholds, then the program provided progressive income redistribution. The benefits for those below the poverty lines may be increased by decreasing the benefits for those above the line, but we do not know who above the line will bear the costs of the additional benefits. Thus this method of adjustment for family size does not provide a good picture of over-all income distribution effects even if net income change is calculated.

Distribution within income groups

So far, programs have been discussed as if they were equally available to all who apply, but in Canada almost all our income transfer programs are 'categorical.'[7] In a categorical program eligibility may be restricted according to demographic characteristics or other criteria such as availability for employment. Even after adjustment for family size, in any categorical program there will be very great differences in the net benefits of individuals within the *same* income class. For example, some single persons in the first income quintile will be over 65 and will receive Old Age Security transfers while some will be under 65 and will not receive transfers. The former will likely have a large net benefit because of the program, while the latter will probably have a small net loss as a result of the tax they bear from the program. Merely recording the average transfer or percentage of transfers for the income class can tell us little. An exaggerated example of this problem would be to depict the income distribution of million dollar lottery winners by the average winning in their (former) income class. Where there is a large 'dispersion in results within each income class, the pattern of mean incidence is not terribly interesting or important ... The tax system is both progressive and regressive' (Thurow 1975, 191).

One method of reporting income distribution results for categorical programs is to estimate the net benefits and net income change for beneficiaries separately from that of non-beneficiaries. The results of moving from a hypothetical Program A to a hypothetical Program B are shown in Table 6. Program A is loosely based on a demogrant, Old Age Security. It is easy to see that separating the benefits of the two groups may result in a very different picture than when they are reported together. For example, the net change in income averaged over the whole income quintile for the program change illustrated in Table 6 is $200, −$225, −$130, −$33, and $118 for the first through the fifth income quintiles respectively compared to $500, −$974, −$1930, −$1895, and −$1763 for beneficiaries and $0, $26, $70, $105, and $237 for non-beneficiaries taken separately. In general, where there is a relatively small number of recipients, reducing the size of the program will mainly benefit non-recipients at the expense of recipients. Non-recipients enjoy tax savings; recipients suffer transfer reductions.

---

7 'Categorical' is sometimes used to mean the same as 'selective.' Here 'categorical' means only that a program will limit eligibility according to criteria other than income or wealth. Thus most universal programs, like Family Allowances and Unemployment Insurance, are also categorical.

TABLE 6
Illustration of effect on income distribution of changing categorical program from universal to selective

| | Quintile | | | | | Total |
	1	2	3	4	5	
No. of families[a] (000,000)	1.6	1.6	1.6	1.6	1.6	8
No. of beneficiaries[b] (000,000)	0.64	0.4	0.16	0.08	0.07	1.35
Financing share[c] %	0	6	16	24	54	100
Program A						
Transfer per beneficiary[d] $	2000	2000	2000	2000	2000	2.7 billion
Average financing burden/ net benefit non-beneficiary[e] $	0	−101	−270	−405	−911	
Net benefit per beneficiary $	2000	1899	1730	1595	1089	2.7 billion
Program B						
Transfer per beneficiary $	2500	1000	0	0	0	
Average financing burden/ net benefit non-beneficiary $	0	−75	−200	−300	−674	
Net benefit per beneficiary $	2500	925	−200	−300	−674	
Net income change Program B − A						
Beneficiary $	500	−974	−1930	−1895	−1763	
Non-beneficiary $	0	26	70	105	237	

a See footnote *a*, Table 3.
b Based on distribution of households with head aged 65+ in 1975, Statistics Canada (1975).
c Based on estimate of direct costs for Old Age Security in Cloutier (1978, 140). Since indirect costs are excluded this probably exaggerates progressivity of financing. Numbers are rounded for easier calculations.
d Total OAS costs in 1975 were $2.6 billion or an average of $1926 per beneficiary family. Since present example is only for illustration, number is rounded to $2000 for a total of $2.7 billion for easier calculation. Based on Statistics Canada (1976).
e Where a program such as OAS is taxable, there will be a dispersion in tax burden within an income class between beneficiaries and others. This is ignored here.

Lifetime income

Both adjusting for family size and distinguishing between beneficiaries and others will critically affect the estimation of the consequences for income distribution. A further problem is whether current money income is an adequate measure for these purposes: for example, low current income may only be a temporary condition. A fuller definition of income, more closely resembling the family's lifetime command over resources, might be a better indication of whether the net benefits of transfer programs are distributed equitably (see Bird and Slack 1978, 65–70, for a review of this question). Of course, the fact that future or past income will be higher may be little consolation to families with low current incomes. Furthermore, it seems plausible that a progressive financing system might 'even out' net benefits on a lifetime basis.

This raises a further complication: namely, if income is to be measured on a lifetime basis, then presumably both transfers and contributions should also be measured on a lifetime basis. This approach seems particularly useful where a program, such as a pension plan, is designed with the intent of changing the flow of income over the life cycle. Indeed it makes little sense to compare the income of those making current contributions in expectation of future transfers to the income of those receiving current transfers and having made contributions in the past. This is the comparison implicit in Cloutier (1978).

Pesando and Rea (1977) take the opposite approach. They analyse the net present value of transfers minus contributions for the Canada Pension Plan. In Rea (1981) Old Age Security and the Guaranteed Income Supplement are also analysed in terms of transfers minus contributions over a lifetime. Rea creates a sample of the probable lifetime histories of various age cohorts in Canada. An age cohort is the group of all persons born in any given year or years. The present value of each family's income is calculated, and families are arranged according to their lifetime income. The present value is equal to the cost of purchasing an annuity to provide the income flow over the period in question. The net wealth in each program is then the present value of benefits minus the present value of contributions (see also Economic Council of Canada 1979, 34–41; Beach 1981).

In a money purchase plan an individual receives the total accumulated value, including interest, of contributions he has made or that have been made on his behalf. This is then used to provide a flow of income during retirement. By definition the net change in wealth in a money purchase plan is zero since the present values are equal. Thus, so long as pensions are organized as money purchase plans there need be no redistribution. Note, however, that in a money purchase plan persons with relatively high incomes could be making current contributions while persons with lower incomes are withdrawing their savings. Looking just at the current income and benefit flows, there would appear to be redistribution from high to low incomes. This appearance is deceptive.

Alternatively, the net wealth for an entire age cohort might sum to zero, but the net wealth for any individual might be positive or negative. In this case there may be redistribution within generations but not between generations. Any fully funded pension will either be of this sort or will be a straight money purchase plan. Again, because current beneficiaries would probably have lower incomes than current contributors, a plan providing regressive redistribution within generations could appear progressive if judged solely on the basis of current flows.

Finally, redistribution between generations will occur where the sum of net wealth for a whole age cohort does not equal zero. Obviously at least some of the individuals' net benefits will then also be non-zero. In pension plans the most common transfer between generations occurs where the net wealth for each succeeding age cohort is positive. In other words, each generation is subsidized by the next. One way to report the distributive effect of this form of pension plan is to estimate the distribution of net wealth among the income groups within each generation. This is the approach taken by Rea (1981), who finds that the Canada Pension Plan is regressive for those currently contributing or benefiting from the plan, but will become progressive if the sum of net wealth for each age cohort gradually falls to zero as the plan matures. The current regressivity of the CPP has occurred at least partly because the current beneficiaries did not have to contribute fully to receive full benefits. The result was a windfall gain that was largest for those with the highest benefits. This finding is opposite to Cloutier (1978, Table 2), who reports that the CPP is progressive. Beach (1981), using a slightly different lifetime approach, also finds that the CPP is regressive. This difference shows the sensitivity of distribution analysis to the use of current or lifetime income.

In the preceding pages it has been argued that the pattern of net benefits, i.e. transfers minus taxes, is what counts in judging the distribution of income. In analysing the distributive consequences of policy *change* it is the difference in net benefits that counts, that is, the change in net income. Furthermore, how one adjusts for family size: whether the change in net benefits for beneficiaries is separated from that for non-beneficiaries; and the definition of income, transfers, and taxes will all substantially affect whether or not a change in policy is viewed as progressive. There are also several other problems of this sort. For example, it is not self-evident what definition of 'family' is appropriate (see Smith et al. 1979, for a discussion of this question) nor even whether it is families rather than individuals that should be considered. 'Income' may include not only non-monetary benefits, such as the imputed rents of owner-occupied housing, but non-tangible benefits as well, such as leisure.

THE INCIDENCE OF TAX-TRANSFER CHANGE

Even if agreement is reached on all the above questions, many others remain. They have to do with the difference between the impact and the ultimate incidence of a change in tax-transfer policy. So far only the immediate impact of tax-transfer policy has been discussed. It has been assumed that those who pay a tax actually bear the burden rather than shifting it onto others and that there are no behavioural changes in response to the new tax-transfer regime. Relaxing these assumptions may affect the distributional outcome. The preceding pages are a discussion of what may be described as 'differential tax–transfer impact analysis.' It looks at the effects of tax-transfer policy, keeping government expenditures on goods and services constant, before shifting of taxes or transfers occurs and assuming no behavioural change as a consequence of the new policy. The next few pages consider the effects of dropping the assumption about tax–transfer shifting and the potential effects of behavioural changes on distribution.

The literature on fiscal incidence offers a number of standard hypotheses about the shifting of taxes and transfers. It is assumed that neither transfers nor income taxes are shifted, but that payroll taxes initially paid by employers fall 100 per cent upon employees. Table 2 assigns only the income tax, including tax paid on the transfer itself, and payroll tax to income classes. In both cases the standard hypotheses are used. It is ordinarily assumed that taxes on items of consumption, including a general sales tax, are borne entirely by consumers of the taxed items. The property tax on buildings is assumed to be shifted onto those who use the services provided in the building – renters or owner-occupiers in the case of the residential property tax. The property tax on land is borne by the land owner. Corporate taxes are split between consumers and owners. (Those are the standard hypotheses presented in Gillespie 1976).

In general the incidence of total taxation will be less progressive than income taxes and payroll taxes alone. Since payroll and income taxes account for about 50 per cent of social security costs (Cloutier 1978), the entire tax–transfer system is probably less progressive than was assumed in deriving Table 2. The incidence of tax reductions is then probably less regressive. Thus, when total tax–transfer incidence is accounted for according to the standard hypotheses, it is less likely that increased transfers to the poor combined with a tax reduction will result in a regressive distribution of changes in net income.

There is, however, continued controversy about these hypotheses. Payroll tax incidence has been the subject of lively debate, and there appears sound reason to doubt that this tax is borne entirely by employees when paid initially by employers (for recent Canadian empirical evidence see Balfour and Beach 1979). The standard assumptions on property tax have been seriously questioned (Bird and Slack 1978). More recently the incidence of the consumption tax has been debated (see Walker 1980 and reply by Wolfson 1980b). Furthermore, transfers may not remain 100 per cent with their direct recipients. Beach (1981) points out that transfers may be shifted either through changes in product prices or through the loss of other transfers. Product prices will change only when beneficiaries of increases in transfers have markedly different baskets of consumption goods than non-beneficiaries. This may be of consequence particularly for services provided specifically to the elderly; for example, some of a pension increase may ordinarily be passed on to nursing home operators or owners of low-rent housing.

The second form of transfer shifting, the loss of one transfer when another is increased, is a planned part of Canada's transfer system. For example the 1974 increases in the Family Allowance were accompanied by decreases in Unemployment Insurance to take account of the additional income available to families. When CPP increases, the Guaranteed Income Supplement and provincial supplements for the elderly automatically decrease by 50 per cent or more of the increased CPP payment. Provincial welfare is ordinarily reduced by 100 per cent of the amount of any other transfers. Although it would be difficult to estimate the precise amount of shifting, it is no doubt extensive and particularly important among the lowest income groups (see the discussion in the Interprovincial Task Force on Social Security 1980).

Ultimately a more general shifting of all transfers and taxes may occur. If the distribution of income mirrors the distribution of power, then any transfer that did succeed in momentarily improving the distribution of income would set off a series of dynamic adjustments, possibly including inflation, until income returned to its previous distribution. Reuber (1978, 527) argues that one possible explanation for the stability of income distribution in Canada is: 'the second-round general equilibrium adjustments in the economy may have offset the distributive policies in the public sector to some extent.' On the other hand, Gillespie argues that government fiscal incidence is not particularly, if at all, redistributive, a possibility also noted by Reuber, so that explanations for its ineffectiveness are hardly required (Gillespie 1976).

The most important types of behavioural changes that may occur as a result of tax–transfer policy relate to work incentives and savings incentives. It is generally agreed that transfers reduce the supply of labour and that taxes are ambiguous in this respect. Economic theory will lead us to predict that part of an increase in transfer payments will be absorbed by an increase in leisure, and that this may not be compensated for by decreased leisure among those bearing the tax burden. On the savings side, public pensions that do not vary according to a recipient's income may replace private savings. Income-tested pensions may reduce private savings by more than the value of the pension, and this may result in an over-all reduction in retirement income for some of the aged. These behavioural changes imply that increases in transfers may not be as effective in improving the distribution of income as impact analysis would predict. Of course, these changes will affect not only the distribution but also the amount of income available to be distributed; this question will be discussed in greater detail below.

There are also other possible behavioural changes of some importance. Fertility may be affected by transfers, particularly if very large benefits are associated with children. Family composition will be affected, as has been shown in income maintenance experiments where the number of families that split up has increased significantly among the treatment groups. Education and the mobility of labour will be affected. It is possible to list several other consequences of changing the tax–transfer programs, most of which will increase the cost of achieving a given income redistribution and decrease the effectiveness of a given tax–transfer change in affecting income redistribution.

In many cases there is very little a government can do or even know about these kinds of tax shifts and behavioural changes. Nevertheless governments have the responsibility of ensuring that the net benefits of changes in taxes and transfers are distributed, at least in their initial impact, according to some concept of equity. In this case tax–transfer impact analysis may be more important for policy purposes than longer run adjustments, which may never be fully understood. Bird and Slack (1978, 85) also come to this conclusion: 'What *is* relevant in many contexts are quantitative estimates of the *impact* (not final incidence, except for the very bold) of *marginal* changes on significant population groups.'

In summary, a system of transfers will probably be less effective and progressive in the long run than in the short run. Behavioural changes are discussed further below in the context of their effect on efficiency. However, there is another aspect of the distributional question in the debate between selectivity and universality that must still be considered. This is the implicit assumption that the only distributional goal of income security programs is to improve the incomes of those who are poorest and, further, that income security programs must have distributional objectives.

OTHER DISTRIBUTIVE OBJECTIVES

Some authors distinguish between an anti-poverty objective and an egalitarian objective in distribution policy (for example, Musgrave 1968). With an anti-poverty goal, transfers are paid to those below a minimum income but the distribution of income is otherwise maintained. An egalitarian objective is concerned with the distribution of income between all classes; transfers may be paid to those above the minimum if greater equality will thereby be achieved. While this distinction may be useful when transfers alone are considered, it is not cogent for the tax–transfer system as a whole. Since taxes will necessarily be collected from those above the minimum, the payment of net benefits to those below the minimum will affect all income. Thus, it is impossible, when pursuing an anti-poverty objective, to follow the advice that 'the prevailing distribution of income is otherwise accepted as proper and not subject to correction' (Musgrave 1968, 25).

However, the redistribution discussed so far in this report, whether called anti-poverty or egalitarian, is mainly 'vertical' or between income groups. Distribution within income groups, called 'horizontal,' may also be an objective of income security programs. Horizontal equity is preserved when people who have the same needs and resources are treated the same way, and those with the same resources but different needs are treated differently. In our tax system, for example, it is generally accepted that those with greater needs should be taxed less. This adjustment is at least partially made through child-related benefits including the Family Allowance, child tax credits, and family-size exemptions in the income tax system. It is easy to see that any tax–transfer system containing provisions for horizontal equity will necessarily contain non-selective elements.

If families with more children should pay less tax, then wealthy families with equal resources but unequal numbers of children should not pay equal tax.

The net reduction in tax may be achieved through a variety of mechanisms,[8] but the net decrease means that some wealthy families will be receiving benefits in the tax–transfer system. If all programs are selective, then wealthy families will not receive any net benefits and horizontal equity will be impossible. Thus some non-selective programs are necessary for this type of equity.

It has been argued so far that income-transfer programs may have two kinds of distributional goals – vertical or horizontal. Greater selectivity may or may not be required for the former objective, depending on the specifics of program design and other factors. The latter objective is incompatible with selectivity. Finally, a third kind of redistribution that society may undertake can be described as the provision of rewards. We may sometimes wish to transfer money to people, not because they need it or because of their income compared to that of others, but only to recognize their past service. Policies for the aged and for veterans may be motivated by this kind of consideration. Of course, taxes will be required to pay those transfers, and they will have distributional effects on all income classes. Presumably those arguing for greater selectivity would also argue that any transfers paid as rewards should be financed progressively. There does not, however, seem to be any reason why society should be denied the right to pay rewards if it so pleases. Such rewards are obviously not related to income.

NON-DISTRIBUTIVE OBJECTIVES

In addition to income distribution there are several other possible reasons for income security programs. These include macro-economic policy, market failure, and risk-pooling in a social insurance program.[9] Each of these reasons and its implications for the universality–selectivity debate is considered briefly below.

Macro-economic policy is concerned with long-term growth, full employment, and stable prices. Payments under income security programs may act

---

8 See Canada (1978) for some interesting examples of the equivalence between different exemption-credit-demogrant schemes. Also see Kesselman (1979) for some interesting alternatives.

9 These are adopted from Bird (1976, 188). In his discussion of unemployment insurance Bird lists four possible reasons for the scheme: stabilization of income and employment; manpower and labour market policy; income maintenance and welfare; and insurance against loss of labour income. The first, second, and third reasons here correspond to Bird's first, second, and fourth respectively. Bird's third reason is of course a distributive objective, which has been discussed above.

as a stabilizer for the economy. If the economy slows down, payments increase and the additional demand helps to boost the economy. Income security programs may also affect savings through forced contribution to funded schemes and the replacement of private savings. However, as Bird (1976) points out, income security programs as we now know them are not required for these purposes; similar results could also be achieved through tax exemptions, direct job creation, or several other alternatives. Although income security programs have macro-economic effects, those must be regarded, not as their primary, but as their secondary purpose. Thus, macro-economic concerns do not appear directly relevant to the universality–selectivity debate, except as a possible side effect of policy change to take into account when reforms are contemplated.

Market imperfections occur when the costs and benefits for the individual cannot be accurately assessed or when these costs do not reflect the harm or good done to others. Market imperfection may occur where the decision-maker, such as a young child, cannot be expected to be competent, where accurate information is unknown or very costly to obtain, and under many other circumstances. Market imperfection is often stated as the reason for specific elements of some programs: for example, unemployment insurance subsidizes job search because a high information cost might otherwise result in less than optimal matches between worker and job. Family Allowance paid to mothers is sometimes seen as a transfer within the family, allowing a woman working in the home a source of independent decision-making she might otherwise not have. The market imperfection in this case is that the economic decisions for the well-being of the family may be dominated by the major bread winner and may not adequately consider the needs and wants of others in the family.

While these considerations may be important in specific cases, market imperfections do not appear to provide a general argument for or against greater selectivity in income security programs. Like macro-economic effects they are secondary consequences warranting attention when new policies are being contemplated, but are not usually the primary objective of a program. One important exception may be costs that are imposed on taxpayers when transfer payments are required by those who could have avoided being in need. This negative externality might justify social insurance so that those with fluctuating incomes would be compelled to protect themselves.[10] Thus,

10 This argument is eloquently made by Musgrave (1968). Rea (forthcoming) argues that the possibility of collecting welfare should not be a justification for compulsory insurance since this is tantamount to making the poor pay for their own welfare.

externalities may relate to the third possible non-distributive goal for income security programs mentioned above, risk-pooling.

It makes sense to insure against many risks. This is because additions to income decrease in importance as income increases. If there is risk that an event may reduce our income we ordinarily want to insure ourselves because the premium paid comes from income that benefits us less than the money we would receive as insurance benefits when our income is lower. But this is only an argument that insurance should be available, not that it should be compulsory.

There are at least three possible reasons for compulsory insurance. First, there may be a cost imposed upon taxpayers if some do not insure themselves, as discussed above. Second, compulsory insurance may be so much cheaper and more efficient, mainly by saving administrative costs, that society as a whole may be better off even though some individuals who would not otherwise have insured themselves may be made worse off. Third, the risks may be such that private insurance is impossible but public compulsory insurance is possible (see Evans and Williamson 1978).

In a perfect insurance program an individual's premium will equal the probability of collecting transfers times the amount of the transfer in the event of collection (assuming neither preference nor aversion to risk). The *ex post* transfer is the amount paid to those collecting a benefit. The expected value of the insurance is the amount of *ex post* transfer times the probability of collecting and this, of course, equals the premium. In a perfect social insurance, the only redistribution will therefore be to those who collect benefits. This form of redistribution should occur on a random basis within each premium group.

In reality, however, there will always be some redistribution before the event since premiums cannot be perfectly tailored to each individual's risk. Moreover, the probability that an event that is insured against will occur will change with time. The probability of collecting at any given time during the life of the insurance contract may therefore not be the same as when the insurance was sold. The gap between probability at the moment of entering into an insurance contract and probability during the life of the contract will increase as the length of the contract increases. If the contract is established before birth, as is essentially done by social insurance schemes, the gap may be very large.

There is no rule that each government program must have only one objective (although there might be good reason to propose such a rule). A social insurance program may deliberately have redistributive elements built into it through adjustment of benefits or of financing (see Chapter 3). This is not unlike any other government program – for example, national defence. We may legitimately enquire as to the income distribution consequences of national defence, and sometimes we may also deliberately build redistribution into our defence programs. But it would be silly to criticize national defence programs for failing to redistribute income to the poor. The point of this paper is not to argue whether or not social insurance programs are in fact necessary; but if they are then it is not reasonable to criticize them for being non-selective.

3
Efficiency and administration

Work incentives, saving incentives, and administration are matters often raised in discussions of the comparative efficiency of universal and selective programs. Work incentives are more precisely defined as changes in labour supply resulting from transfers. It has generally been agreed that demogrants will have the least effect on work incentives (see Lampman 1978), but there has been no direct comparison between social insurance and income-related programs with respect to labour supply. Moreover the net benefits of most demogrants are related to income and are therefore similar to selective programs. It will be argued here that the difference in the labour supply effects of universal and selective programs is minimal and unpredictable.

Public pensions may affect personal saving by reducing the need to save for retirement. For the elderly there is a possibility of a net benefit largely unrelated to income because the tax burden upon recipients will be small. While theory predicts that pensions related to income may decrease personal saving more than other types of transfer programs, empirical evidence is still unavailable. However the decrease in personal saving may be more than offset by increases from other sources.

Turning finally to the question of administration: administrative costs are lower for demogrants than for other programs, but the differences are modest. Programs may also differ in their administrative flexibility, since the responsiveness to change in income and the intrusiveness of the system may be critically affected by whether or not programs are selective. Gains and losses in administrative flexibility may be more important than differences in administrative cost.

WORK INCENTIVES

The labour-leisure trade-off

If the gain from an hour of labour is the wage rate and if the price of leisure is the wage forgone when not working, then there is a trade-off between labour and leisure. Imagine a job where the wage rate is given but there is complete flexibility in the number of hours worked. The worker's decision about how long to work will reflect his relative preference for income and for the time in which to enjoy it. If a tax–transfer program changes either the wage rate or income, then the worker will generally want to spend either more or less time working. The desire to change the amount of time spent working is known as the 'incentive' effect of the program.

The labour–leisure trade-off may be affected either by a change in unearned income, or by a change in the wage rate. Imagine for example that our hypothetical worker earns $5 an hour and decides to work 40 hours a week. Now we give him an unearned income of $50 a week (paid for by someone else). Will he continue to work forty hours a week or will he work less, take a smaller increase in income, and have more leisure time? It is usually believed that the latter is more likely, and that part of an increase in unearned income will be 'absorbed' by an increase in leisure. But if our imaginary worker's salary goes up to $6 an hour, the increase in income that is possible at the higher wage rate and the desire to consume more leisure are offset by the increased price of leisure, because every hour taken off will now cost a dollar more in lost wages.

We can see therefore that the net result of an increase in the wage rate is not predictable: there are two opposing influences, and theory does not tell us which is larger. But if there is a lump-sum increase in income (paid for by someone else), the direction of the incentive is predictable and will result in increased leisure. But a selective transfer program can *lower* the effective wage rate while at the same time increasing income. Thus there will be no offsetting effect and it can therefore be predicted in theory that a decrease in the desired number of hours worked will result.

To illustrate how a selective transfer program can accomplish the apparently miraculous feat of simultaneously reducing effective wage rates and increasing income, turn once more to our hypothetical worker. Imagine that he is working forty hours a week at $5 an hour. Now we introduce a selective program paying a maximum of $200 a week to anyone who has no income at all, but the transfer is then reduced by 50¢ for every $1 of other income. Someone with $400 a week will get no transfers at all. Assuming that our worker does not have to help finance this program, he will now have an income of $300 a week if he continues to work 40 hours. But since he would have $200 if he did no work, his gain from those 40 hours is now only $100, or $2.50 an hour. Because the marginal tax rate on each dollar of earnings up to $400 is 50 per cent, his effective (net) wage rate has decreased while at the same time his income has increased.

With an income-related net benefit, both the lower wage rate and the increase in income combine to encourage additional leisure, but with a flat net benefit, as in a demogrant without an associated tax burden, there is only one inducement to increased leisure. For this reason it is usually argued that, other things being equal, the reduction in work effort will be greater with a selective program than with a demogrant.

Quantitative estimates
Under the assumption of no associated tax burden, there have been numerous estimates of the reduction in labour supply expected as a result of various selective programs, as well as social insurance programs. These have included several social experiments with control groups. Unfortunately, the data for the one Canadian experiment, The Manitoba Basic Annual Income Experiment, although collected, have not yet been analysed. However, according to the American experiments, the labour supply reduction from a completely non-categorical selective program would probably be only about 2.5 per cent for the labour force as a whole but about 12 per cent for recipients.[11]

There have been no experiments to measure the work disincentives of social insurance. Measurements have instead been based on econometric analysis and have been restricted almost entirely to Unemployment Insurance. Jump and Rea (1975) argue that the incentive effects of UI are similar to those of a selective program if there is restricted time in which accumulated benefits may be collected; if the time horizon is unrestricted then the effects are closer to those of a lump-sum transfer. They also point out that a period of work is required to become eligible for benefits. This therefore increases labour-force participation and the supply of labour since wages are effectively increased by the accumulation of future entitlements. Furthermore, UI maintains the demand for goods and services in periods of high unemployment, so that with UI employment is higher than it would otherwise be. Although increased demand is also present in selective programs, it is usually ignored (exceptions are Swan et al. 1976, Golladay and Haveman

11 These figures are from estimates by Masters and Garfinkel (1977). See Hum (1980) for a review of the experiments, also Keeley et al. 1978.

1977). Because of the multiplicity of conflicting effects there remains a great deal of controversy about the amount of decrease in work effort, if any.[12]

The literature cited above suffers from two serious limitations. First, labour supply effects are usually discussed as if all programs were non-categorical. Second, theoretical and empirical labour supply estimates are based on gross transfers rather than net benefits. Since programs are assumed to be non-categorical, benefits are treated as if they are available to anyone without test of employability. In fact, most proposals for expanded selective programs in Canada include employment availability testing as a condition of eligibility (for example, Canada 1973), and most politically acceptable schemes will require the beneficiaries to prove that they are available for work. This regulation will affect the work-leisure trade-off by restricting the choice available, and will decrease the predicted negative impact on work incentives. The studies often do not adequately take into account the existence of a work test, particularly in their micro-economic theory (Jump and Rea 1975, Kesselman 1971 are exceptions).

The second and more important point is that there is *no* theoretical distinction between demogrant and selective programs in terms of labour supply response. This is because neither selective programs nor demogrants provide a flat *net* benefit unadjusted for income. As seen in the discussion of income distribution, programs that pay flat rate gross transfers may turn out to have progressive net benefits. Since labour-supply is affected by net benefits, there is no qualitative distinction between the effects of selective and demogrant programs on labour supply. This view is substantiated by Kesselman and Garfinkel (1978), who take into account the financing burden associated with income security programs and simulate the distortions caused by the *net* benefits for demogrants compared to selective programs. They find that the differences are very small. Betson, Greenberg, and Kasten (1981) estimate labour-supply effects based on net benefits. As expected, they find that we cannot foresee whether a demogrant will have more or less influence on labour supply than a selective program. Which has less effect depends on the precise details of the programs being compared.

Increasing the selectivity of demogrants
In Canada we are interested in the effects of a marginal increase in the selectivity of current demogrants. If we take transfers paid under a non-categorical demogrant and channel them more selectively to the poor, and if we do not at the same time decrease the total amount of transfers paid out or

---

12 See Hum (1981) for a review of the literature on Canadian unemployment insurance.

change the tax system, then the net benefits of the program will be concentrated more fully on lower-income families than under the demogrant. At the same time, marginal tax rates will increase among those receiving positive net benefits so that effective wage rates will decrease. Both effects are likely to result in less work effort among the poor. But the decrease in net benefits among the wealthy implies a positive effect with respect to work effort. Whether the increases in work effort would outweigh the losses remains an empirical question. The results of the last two studies cited above suggest that the total net difference in work effort will be quite small.

If a non-categorical demogrant is made more selective but the total transfers paid out are also reduced, then the wealthy as well as the poor may expect an increase in net benefits, paid for by a decrease in the net benefits of the middle-income group. Also, the marginal tax rates paid by both the middle-income and wealthy groups may decrease. Thus, the net effect on the poor is to decrease their work effort, and on the middle-income group to increase their work effort; the effect on the wealthy is not predictable in theory. Again, the total result is unknown.

Of course, Canada's two demogrants, Family Allowances and Old Age Security, are categorical so that in each income class there are non-recipients as well as recipients. Work incentives affect individuals, not averages in an income class. If a categorical demogrant is made more selective but there is no change in total transfers or the tax system, then non-recipients will remain unaffected by the change. However, if there is a reduction in total spending, then incomes will increase while marginal tax rates will decrease for non-recipients. Thus, non-recipients are affected, although the net direction of the effect is not known. In summary, whenever a demogrant is made more selective there are always offsetting factors so that we cannot foresee the aggregate effect on work effort. Furthermore, the aggregate change will probably be small.

Increasing the selectivity of social insurance programs
If a social insurance program is necessary, it may be reasonable to use it to try to achieve the secondary objective of income redistribution. There are several ways redistribution can be accomplished, such as by special benefits (regional benefits in UI, dependants' benefits in the CPP/QPP) or through subsidy of contributions either from general revenue or within the program. All of these adjustments reduce the efficiency gains from the program, but this may be a justifiable cost in light of society's redistributive aims.

The change in social insurance most often proposed is to increase redistribution by imposing special income-related surtaxes on the transfers paid.

These would be over and above taxes paid according to the ordinary tax schedule, where transfers are treated like any other income subject to tax. In UI the effect on incentives will be complicated because there is a period in which entitlement is accumulated as well as a period when it may be collected. Rea (1977) argues that the result of making UI taxable in 1972 was to increase work effort, and it is reasonable to expect a surtax to accentuate this result. But Rea does not take into account the reduced tax subsidies from general revenue. There is therefore an offsetting effect reducing work effort.

Another way of increasing the redistributive effect of a social insurance program is to reduce contributions for those with lower incomes. This is done in UI by paying part of the costs from general revenue (assuming that general revenue is progressive). This increases marginal tax rates, decreases income for the wealthy, and increases income for the poor. The net effect on work incentives is unknown. Among those who receive a payment from UI, the distribution of net benefits with an increase in the selectivity of transfers may be identical to the distribution of net benefits with an increase in the selectivity of contributions. But the expected value of the insurance (the probability of collecting times the amount paid in the event of collecting) cannot be identical since changes in contributions affect everyone, but changes in transfers affect only those actually collecting. It seems, other things being equal, that making transfers rather than contributions more selective would probably reduce work incentives less.

While taxing transfers may therefore be the superior method from the point of view of work incentives, there are a number of other problems associated with any surtax (over and above the tax that would result from treating transfer income the same way as other income). First, the administration of such special taxes is complex and probably intrusive. Second, such a proposal means that the wealthier unemployed will finance the poorer unemployed instead of the wealthy subsidizing the poor in general. Just as an income-tested health deterrent fee is a tax on the sick (Barer, Evans, and Stoddart 1979), so the income-testing of unemployment benefits is a tax on the unemployed. Finally, one must question the fairness of singling out this particular form of income for special treatment. Why are unemployment transfers more deserving of surtaxes than interest payments, capital gains, and other forms of income? This and other proposals to increase the selectivity of social insurance are discussed in Chapter 5.

In summary, the net effect on work incentives of increasing the selectivity of demogrants is not predictable in theory. Whether a demogrant or a selective program will have the least negative impact on work incentives depends upon the details of the programs being compared. Making a social insurance program more selective will probably have less influence on work effort if it is done through transfers rather than contributions, but there are a number of objections on other grounds. In total, the difference in work incentives turns out to be small and thus not very important in the debate between universality and selectivity. Can the same be said for saving incentives?

SAVINGS INCENTIVES

Protection against fluctuations in income or need and the provision of income in retirement are among the many reasons for a family to save a part of its income, but social security programs that provide protection and retirement income will diminish the importance of those savings. Since the need to save is reduced, it is often argued that savings will also decrease. Moreover, when transfer benefits are selective, the income from private savings will be of less benefit because private income will result in reduced transfers. Thus, in the case of non-selective programs, transfers may replace income from private savings; while in the case of selective programs, income from private savings may not only be replaced but the total may also be reduced.

These two effects are similiar to the effects on work effort described above. Imagine the life cycle is divided in two periods – before and after retirement. A person would ordinarily wish to ensure a reasonable flow of income in both periods. If there is no other income after retirement, then some income from before retirement would have to be saved for later. If government transfers provide income in the second period, then less money will need to be saved from the first period. Thus part of increased income in the second period is 'absorbed' by increased consumption in the first period.

When the transfer is selective it also changes the rate at which savings will be of benefit in the second period. A dollar of savings may no longer provide a dollar of benefits in the second period if increases in income result in decreases in transfers. In the extreme, if there is a dollar reduction in transfers for each dollar of income in the second period, there is no reason to save anything at all unless one can save more than the total transfers available. For those with low income, there is now a confiscatory tax of this kind because of the 100 per cent tax rate created by many provincial elderly supplement programs. Even with only the 50 per cent rate in the Guaranteed Income Supplement (GIS), anyone who in the absence of the selective program would have saved enough to provide income between the minimum guarantee up to a little more than the cut-off[13] (about \$4800 for a single person in November 1980) would likely now reduce their saving so that their *total* income in the second period would actually be less (see Kesselman 1981b).

As usual, there are a number of factors offsetting the clear-cut theoretical conclusion that personal savings will be reduced. First, the public pension may encourage earlier retirement, so that the increase in income is absorbed not by decreased savings but by increased leisure. This may even lead to an increase in savings so as to provide sufficient income during a longer retirement (Feldstein 1974). Second, parents may take advantage of the increased second-period income to provide greater bequests to their children (Barro 1974). Or, children may decrease their voluntary transfers to their parents and save part of that money. Finally, families may aim for a minimum target income, particularly during the working years, in which case an increase in income is converted almost entirely into a hedge against falling below the minimum income and very little value is attached to going above the minimum. If this is true, then any income above the minimum will be saved regardless of the public program.

Similar arguments about changes in private saving can be made for other transfers, such as Unemployment Insurance. The theoretically predictable effect of transfers on personal savings is ambiguous, but if there is a negative effect it is likely to be larger for selective than non-selective programs. However, this applies only to an individual's personal savings which may in turn be more than offset by other sources of savings.

Obviously, one important alternative source will be the compulsory saving taking place in funded social security schemes. For those who would have saved less than the amount they save through compulsory contributions, total savings are increased. Where these contributions only offset private savings which would have otherwise been made, there is no change in total saving. Of course not all transfer schemes are funded and not all funds are actually 'saved' as some may be used to finance current consumption of goods and services. Even if the total of all personal saving, both compulsory and voluntary, decreases, there still may be no effect since it may be offset by higher corporate saving. And none of this need have any effect on investment since a decline in domestic investment may be fully compensated for

---

13 Rea (1974) shows that those with income that would have been above a break-even point in the absence of a program may also be affected by the incentives of the program. How far beyond the break-even point this extends will depend upon the individual's preferences. See also Kesselman (1971).

by an increase in foreign investment. Theory, therefore, not only fails to predict the change in personal savings, but it also fails to predict what the change in aggregate savings will be and why we should be concerned about it in the first place. The only thing theory tells us clearly is that *if* there is any effect on personal saving, it is likely to be greater in selective programs.[14]

With respect to work incentives I have argued that programs did not pay a true flat benefit, because net benefits were progressive even in the case of an apparent demogrant such as the family allowance. Therefore, one cannot foresee how the incentive effects of supposedly non-selective will differ from those of selective programs. This is also true with respect to savings incentives for a program where beneficiaries are a significant proportion of the population. But, as discussed above, where recipients are relatively few, the importance of the tax burden diminishes in relation to transfer benefits (simply because the recipient population bears only a small portion of the tax burden). Thus, for recipients of such a benefit there is some possibility of an almost true demogrant, that provides flat net benefits. This is illustrated in Table 6 by program A, using numbers approximating the existing Old Age Security program. Thus, in the case of the elderly it is possible to have 'real' demogrant programs and to distinguish their incentive effects on the elderly from those of selective programs.[15] Of course, the incremental tax borne by the non-elderly may itself cause offsetting behaviour.

Unfortunately, there is not yet any good empirical evidence about the effect on saving of various types of programs. This is because it is very difficult to separate all the influences on the rate of personal saving. An attempt was made by the Ontario Treasury Department to distinguish the effects of OAS from the Canada and Quebec Pension Plans. One of the models they test shows that the OAS has 'no net effect on the personal saving rate ... [but] the CPP and QPP lowered the rate of personal saving' (Ontario 1979, 28). However, the paper acknowledges that there are a number of severe limitations to the data and there also appear to be some methodological problems, so that the results must be regarded with caution. In any event, since both these programs are non-selective, these results would still not be of much use in resolving the universality versus selectivity debate. Furthermore the Ontario paper does not consider the effects of the incremental tax

14 See ECC (1979) for a review of the effect of pension schemes on saving. Also see Pesando and Rea (1977).
15 Where only a small proportion of the population is receiving benefits, there can be a similar a priori distinction between the work incentive effects of selective and demogrant programs, but most programs directed towards those in the labour force are much more general.

burden. Other empirical studies in Canada[16] also appear unable to distinguish between the effects of selective and non-selective programs.

In summary, we do not know if there is a reduction in personal savings, and there is no evidence yet whether one type of program diminishes personal savings more than any other. The issue of savings incentives therefore remains undecided so far as the debate addressed in this paper is concerned, although there is a theoretical argument that the effects of selective programs are larger. Further light may be shed on this issue with more empirical research in the future.

ADMINISTRATION

It is popularly believed that the current array of transfer programs is very expensive to administer. When over-all welfare reform was first discussed in the United States, a reduction in supposedly high administrative cost was used as an argument for replacing the existing system with a negative income tax (Friedman 1962). This same argument is occasionally made to-day (Crispo 1979). There are two assumptions implicit in this approach: first, that administrative costs are a large proportion of total costs; and second, that a negative income tax or similar selective scheme will reduce these costs. Both these assumptions are questionable.

The administrative costs as a percentage of total costs for six income security programs are presented in Table 7. Only the relatively small municipal allowance program had administrative costs greater than 10 per cent of total costs. It is not the selective programs but the demogrants that have the lowest administrative costs. This is true not only of administration as a percentage of total costs, but also of administration costs per case. Administrative costs for the demogrant Family Allowance were estimated to be about $2 per case in 1976–7, while those for the Guaranteed Income Supplement (GIS) were approximately $15 per case (Mendelson 1979, 86). The GIS is as inexpensive administratively as any selective program could ever be: income is retroactively reported on the basis of the previous year's tax return, there are no work tests or any other eligibility requirements beyond age and residence, and the elderly as a group have exceptionally stable incomes. Social insurance schemes come in third: the Canada Pension Plan's cost per case was about $47 in 1975.[17] However, the most expensive of all are selective pro-

16 As reported in ECC (1979).
17 From Statistics Canada (1976, Tables 7 and 10). An estimate derived by dividing administrative cost by the total number of beneficiaries in the year.

TABLE 7
Administrative costs as a percentage of total cost for
six income security programs in 1975–6 fiscal year

Canada			Ontario		
Family Allowance	Old Age (OAS & GIS)	Unemployment Insurance	Workmen's Compensation	Prov. social assistance	Munic. social assistance
0.5	0.45	5.5	8.4	4.2	14.7
			(1975)	(1972–3)	

SOURCE: Mendelson (1979)

grams with complex determination of eligibility and benefits. The needs-tested provincial assistance program had costs per case of almost $130 in 1976–7 dollars (ibid., 25).

Unfortunately those measures are very imperfect. While demogrants may have the lowest costs per case, they also have the largest number of cases. As well, demogrants will pay a greater sum of gross transfers, but not necessarily net benefits, and consequently their administrative costs will almost certainly be a lower percentage of total costs than selective programs. These results do not seem very meaningful. What is needed instead is a measure of administrative cost in relation to net benefits. In other words, what does it cost to redistribute, not just to distribute?

To answer this question we might compare the administrative costs of two different types of reform for the whole tax–transfer system. One type of reform is the familiar negative income tax (NIT). The NIT extends the income tax into the 'negative' ranges so that as income decreases an increasing transfer is paid, up to some maximum for those with no income. Another approach to reform is the credit income tax (CIT), which would terminate all exemptions in the income tax, provide a refundable credit for everyone, and institute a flat tax rate for all income brackets, (see Kesselman 1981b for a more complete description of the CIT and the NIT). The NIT is selective; the CIT is universal. For a given amount of redistribution would an NIT or a CIT be more expensive to administer?

The CIT's cost per case will definitely be lower, but there will be many more cases (indeed everyone will be a 'case'). Despite this, an educated guess is that the CIT would be less expensive to administer because it could be more fully integrated into the tax system and the 'positive' tax system itself would become less expensive to administer. As is discussed more fully below, an NIT, aside from its appealing name, cannot be well integrated into the ordinary tax system and it requires a great deal of separate administration.

In Canada, however, wholesale reform of the tax–transfer system does not appear to be on the political agenda. It is more likely that there will be marginal changes in the existing system. We might then ask whether making some of the present universal programs more selective will result in an increase or decrease in administrative costs. Unfortunately there does not seem to be a single answer to this question. Some marginal increases in selectivity will probably decrease costs, whereas others will probably increase them. For example, because the GIS already exists and provides benefits to over 55 per cent of those receiving OAS, shifting all OAS payments to the GIS would probably save some administrative costs. On the other hand, the shift of family allowance to the RCTC probably resulted in an increase in administrative cost because the RCTC was a new program that required a new income tax form and the old family allowance remains with no lower administrative costs. In short, the administrative costs of new policies would have to be examined case by case.

Whatever the changes in administrative cost, they are likely to be small compared to the flow of transfer payments through government. In other words, administration is and will remain a small proportion of total transfers. But unlike transfers, administration is an appropriation of resources by the public sector. If administration therefore represents a 'real' cost, while transfers do not, perhaps we should be more concerned about the over-all size of the former and less concerned about the latter. Total administrative costs for the whole income security system were probably about $500 million in 1978–9. Replacing the whole system with a CIT would probably involve administrative costs of about $50 million. An NIT might cost about $200 million. If there were categorical treatment of recipients in either of these programs, there would be additional costs. Thus about $150 million or less is the administrative burden governments must carry to minimize expenditures when these include the flow of transfers through government (figures from Mendelson 1979).

There are, however, aspects of administration other than costs to the government that may be more important in choosing between types of programs. These include the administrative capacity to deliver the right amount of benefits when they are needed by eligible recipients, and with a minimum of inconvenience or interference. The extent to which a program can meet these objectives depends upon its design. There are several criteria, other than cost to government, that may be useful for evaluating the administration of income security programs. They are maximum responsiveness, minimum intrusiveness and compliance cost for recipients, minimum collection of overpayments, maximum participation among those eligible, flexible definitions of income, and minimum stacking of tax rates. While there are many more criteria, this list may be used to survey some possible administrative consequences of greater or lesser selectivity.

Responsiveness
Responsiveness is the ability of a program 'to adjust benefits rapidly when changes in income occur' (Canada 1975, 41). Many of our present selective programs are highly unresponsive. When the income test is based on the income tax system, the payment is adjusted according to last year's income, which may bear little resemblance to current needs. Many negative income tax experiments as well as one Canadian income-tested program, the Saskatchewan Family Income Plan, have attempted to base payments on more current income, but this has involved extraordinarily complex reporting systems and often the repayment of large over-payments in a year-end reconciliation period. (See Hum et al. 1979, Crest et al. 1979, and Billet et al. 1979 for a good example of what is required to achieve responsiveness in a selective program while maintaining other objectives. See Saskatchewan (1976) for an assessment of an operational selective program attempting to remain responsive.)

On the other hand, our existing demogrants make transfer payments regardless of income. But whether or not an individual remains a net beneficiary will depend on whether the incremental tax burden is adjusted in a timely fashion. In the current system the adjustment of tax withholding provides some responsiveness. However there is no withholding on many forms of income, and as a result tax burdens may accumulate to the end of the year. But since for anyone in need the tax burden should be small, this unresponsiveness of demogrants appears less troublesome than that of existing selective programs. Moreover, the tax withholding system is designed so that there is usually a repayment from the government rather than to the government. Kesselman (1981b) argues persuasively that an NIT would be much less responsive than a CIT.

Intrusiveness and compliance cost for recipients
As noted above, a selective program becomes extremely complicated if it attempts to remain responsive, invariably requiring special income reporting forms for recipients. The forms may be simple if there is great reliance on the reconciliation period, or they may be much more detailed in order to mini-

mize reconciliations at the end of the year. In the latter case there will be a large burden on the recipients: forms, interviews, and sometimes line-ups. In the former case there will be reduced responsiveness and probably political problems when repayments are necessary (Saskatchewan 1976).

Perhaps more important than line-ups is the interference with, and humiliation of, applicants[18] that may be part of a selective program. This can include and has included everything from regulation of sexual habits to rules about how often eyeglasses can be replaced. Such interference is most common in provincial and municipal social assistance. Many decisions that adults of almost any nation take for granted as being their personal prerogative are the subject of bureaucratic regulation for 'welfare' recipients – just because they are recipients and not as a result of an assessment of special social need. Although this situation is certainly improving, it remains a feature of Canada's main selective program: social assistance. The potential for such abuse is much higher in selective than universal programs. Kesselman (1981a) reviews compliance costs and intrusiveness in much greater detail. He also concludes that these problems are more likely to occur in selective programs.

Of course, where there are selective programs already in existence, such as the Refundable Child Tax Credit, marginal changes towards increased selectivity should impose no more burden on recipients if the existing delivery system can accommodate larger payments. Thus the argument that selective programs impose burdens on recipients may only be relevant to larger changes where one program is actually replacing another and a whole delivery system can be reformed. Although non-selective programs are simpler and impose smaller compliance costs on recipients, the above argument applies equally to marginal changes towards non-selectivity. There will be no gains in terms of reduced complexity and compliance costs unless the change is large enough to allow a whole delivery system to be replaced.

Overpayment collection

In any program where there are increasing marginal tax rates, including the positive tax system, the timing of income can be important. This is because two small amounts will be taxed differently than their sum. For this reason there is usually some method of income averaging, most often over a year. The amount actually paid, usually on a monthly basis, must then be recon-

---

18 Compliance and intrusiveness are often seen as the same as 'stigma.' In this study, stigma is treated as something that happens *in* a person rather than *to* a person. Thus a humiliating experience may cause stigma, but it is not the same as stigma. Stigma is discussed further in Chapter 4.

ciled against the amount that should have been paid out on the basis of average yearly income. Where the former is greater than the latter this is known as an overpayment. Collecting overpayments may cause hardship and will be politically difficult.

Various methods have been devised to minimize overpayments in selective programs. In the extreme, they are simply eliminated by basing payment on current income and not averaging income. This means that there will be inequity among recipients: those having variable income often receive higher payments. Another method is to base payments on a floating average, but while this reduces the effect of fluctuations in income, it also decreases the responsiveness of the program. Finally, payments may be based on retroactive income, thereby obviating the need to reconcile, but as pointed out above, this substantially reduces the responsiveness of the program.

Non-selective programs will have a similar problem in assigning the incremental tax burden if there is an increasing marginal tax rate in the positive tax system. In this case, the problem is caused by underpayments of tax during the year rather than overpayments of transfers. This could be minimized by increased tax-withholding. As well, the incremental tax burden, unlike the repayment of overpayments in selective programs, is relatively greater for those with higher incomes. A full-scale CIT would entail constant marginal tax rates, and therefore would have the very great advantage of entirely removing any tax benefit or loss associated with fluctuations in income. Of course, the timing of the tax payment may still not coincide with the timing of the income receipt unless there is perfect tax withholding (Kesselman, 1981b).

Participation among those eligible
To be equitable a program must not only treat all participants fairly, but it must also ensure that there is full take-up of the program among all those eligible. Demogrants usually have a very high participation rate; selective programs have lower participation rates. In the Manitoba NIT experiment, participation rates varied from 50 per cent to over 90 per cent. The latter rate was found among single heads of families in the saturation site, a small town where every resident was eligible (Sabourin and Hum 1979).

One of the few studies of take-up rates for Canadian income security programs was done for the Old Age Security and Guaranteed Income Supplement. OAS was found to have full take-up. However, for GIS 'the recipient take-up rate is in the 80% to 85% range for all of Canada' (Beavis and Kapur 1977, 33). A more recent study by Chan and Hum (1980) finds that participation rates are significantly lower among the Chinese minority in Canada.

Since the GIS is straightforward and non-intrusive, the Beavis and Kapur findings are probably a more realistic upper limit for enrolment on selective programs than the saturation site in Manitoba, where a significant effort was made to obtain enrolment. While the 1977 study argues that publicity in 1972 also helped boost enrolment in the GIS, it concludes that further efforts would probably not yield equal results since many of those eligible but not participating are entitled to only small tranfers.

It is not certain whether many small inequities are better than a few large inequities. If 200,000 pensioners fail to enrol for a few dollars more a month (Beavis and Kapur 1977, 22), is this a successful take-up rate? This remains a matter of opinion. It is clear, however, that demogrants, if not universal programs as a whole, will have higher take-up rates than selective programs.

Definition of income
There is no administrative reason why a full-scale NIT or CIT need be restricted in its definition of income, although the equity of either plan will be seriously affected by the definition of income. However, in considering incremental shifts in our current system, problems surrounding the definition of income may crucially affect plans for greater selectivity. The income tax system is the only existing administrative mechanism for income-testing the whole population. But the income tax system has several features that may be unacceptable for transfer programs. These include the retroactive reporting of income, the partial or complete exemption of certain forms of income such as capital gains and imputed income from home ownership, and the taxation of personal rather than family income (see Canada 1978).

If the reduction rate on a selective program is applied to income as defined through the income tax system, anomalies will appear (although to no worse degree than in the tax system). For example, persons with very substantial capital may be entitled to payments whereas wage earners with smaller incomes but little personal wealth may be denied payments. This, along with the requirement for large repayment of overpayments, was the main problem encountered in Saskatchewan. On the other hand, if special amendments are made to the tax system just to handle the transfer program, the tax system may be compromised, and may also become much more cumbersome. This has been seen in the administration of the Refundable Child Tax Credit, which requires the submission and handling of a separate form. If an acceptable definition of income requires a whole new income-testing system, this would offset whatever administrative gain had been expected from the move to greater selectivity.

Of course, existing demogrant programs suffer from much the same problem since net beneficiaries will be determined by the tax system. A person with substantial wealth but little personal income may turn out to be a net beneficiary, while a wage earner with little wealth turns out to be a net payer. This simply reflects whatever unfairness is inherent in the tax system. One suspects that this inequity is more acceptable only because it is more difficult to detect. Nevertheless, incremental moves to greater selectivity may require new administrative machinery if the definition of income is to be politically acceptable.

Stacking of tax-back rates
There are numerous programs where the amount of benefit or tax paid depends upon the economic resources of the recipients. In Ontario, these include the positive tax system, subsidized Ontario health insurance premiums, provincial tax credits, and, for some, Family Benefits Allowance and subsidized housing and day care. The rate at which benefits decrease as income increases may 'stack up' over all these programs. The result may be tax-back rates of 100 per cent or more where a recipient is actually made worse off by increasing earned income (Ontario Economic Council 1979, 64).

With a full NIT or CIT, many of these programs would be integrated into the main tax–transfer program and stacking would be minimized. However, incremental increases in selectivity may aggravate the problem of stacking without providing an opportunity for integration. Even the 5 per cent tax-back rate on the Refundable Child Tax Credit adds significantly to the marginal tax rates of middle-income families paying income tax. The surtax on unemployment insurance transfers may add further to marginal tax rates if the family has collected any UI.

The problem of stacking is shared by proposals to increase demogrants and apply special surtaxes to them (for example, Quebec 1971; more recently, Kapsalis 1980). Presumably a surtax is believed to be necessary because the positive tax system is not progressive enough or because it is politically inexpedient to increase positive taxes. The surtax will stack with the positive tax system and other programs in exactly the same way as would a more direct selective program.

The above has been a very brief survey of some administrative issues in the debate between selectivity and universality. Other criteria include the definition of the family unit, the minimization of avoidance behaviour, the maximization of understanding of the program, and doubtless many other points. There are two tentative conclusions suggested from the above discussion. First, administrative problems associated with incremental change are often different from those arising from over-all reform through the introduction of a general NIT or CIT. Second, there are some difficulties inherent in incremental moves towards greater selectivity. These are decreased responsiveness, increasingly complex administration possibly accompanied by somewhat higher costs, decreased participation rates, and more pronounced stacking of marginal taxes.

4
Social and institutional factors

The universality–selectivity question may be pursued within several distinct academic traditions. Economists usually discuss the distributional effects and efficiency of income security programs. However, non-economists have also played a role in the design and operation of programs. Social workers have addressed the universality–selectivity debate from the point of view of social relationships, and political scientists have looked at the policy-making apparatus and our political institutions. These points of view are the subject of this chapter.

The stigmatizing of recipients has been a central argument against selective programs. Since persons singled out for assistance may begin to see themselves as less capable and less worthy human beings, selective programs may contribute to the continuation of poverty by convincing the poor that they are fit for nothing better. In the last few years, advances in administrative design have apparently lessened the stigma of selective programs. But whether these techniques are useful for reducing stigma in more extensive selective programs remains in question. Drawing on the discussion of stigma, selective programs are also believed to divide society and result in a loss of 'social cohesion.'

This chapter also considers the effects of universality and selectivity on federalism. Canada's federal political organization has been central to the design of our social security system. The distribution of powers and the co-ordination of programs may be vitally affected by a move toward greater selectivity. In turn, the possibility of any reform of income security will partially depend upon its effect on intergovernmental relations.

STIGMA

Do selective programs stigmatize?
The problem of stigma has played a decisive role in the development of Canada's income security system. For example, universal Old Age Security payments were introduced in 1951 mainly to end the 'close and recurring scrutiny of a pensioner's personal affairs' implicit in the means testing of pensions (Bryden 1974, 104). In 1970 the federal government's white paper on income security noted that 'the stigma of poor relief and the dole still lingers and is often reinforced by humiliating procedures and policies' (Canada 1970, 36). *The Working Paper on Social Security* (Canada 1973) sees stigma as one of the 'deficiencies' of the current system that reform should address.

A stigma sets an individual apart from the rest of the community. According to Williamson (1974, 213), 'those who are stigmatized have attributes, either alleged or real, that detract from their character and reputation making it difficult for others to relate to them in a normal way.' All selective programs will use a test of means or income. 'The fundamental objective of all such tests of eligibility is to keep people out; not to let them in. They must, therefore, be treated as applicants or supplicants; not beneficiaries or consumers ... [The test then fosters] both the sense of personal failure and the stigma of a public burden' (Titmuss 1968, 134).

Some authors use 'stigma' to refer to humiliation or investigation in the process of testing. Others see it as identification by the individual and society that may occur as a result of the testing. In this paper the intrusiveness of the system and the humiliation of applicants are treated mainly as compliance costs. Stigma is seen here as a more long-lasting phenomenon whose effects may be felt many years after a recipient has undergone whatever rigors are involved in a test. To be stigmatized is to be identified by one's self and by others as a 'loser.'

In the last few years there has been less concern about stigma, because it now appears possible to deliver benefits with less odious administrative methods. For example, the Canadian Council on Social Development argues that 'by using the income tax system ... the stigma and administrative cost normally associated with welfare programs will be avoided' (CCSD 1979, 9). There are at least two ways in which the income tax system may be 'used.' One way is to use the system as the test on which to base selective payments. Another is to increase tax rates so that those with more income will have lower or negative net benefits. Obviously, demogrants will have no stigma, but will the use of income tax for testing reduce the stigma of selective programs? Experience with the Guaranteed Income Supplement (GIS) appears to confirm that a selective program will have little stigma if testing is done through the income tax system. There is no popular portrayal of GIS recipients as 'failures.'

In the GIS, application is made by a simple, mail-in form. There is no face-to-face interview. There are no provisions for testing assets, and the income test is applied through the regular income tax system based on last year's income. But extrapolating from the GIS experience to claim that further increases in selectivity will be equally benign involves two assumptions – that a similar method of testing could be employed in achieving greater selectivity and that the *method* of testing is what makes GIS non-stigmatizing.

As argued above, the testing techniques used by GIS may not be applicable to more extensive selective programs. It is likely that the income of the elderly is unusually constant from year to year. Even for the elderly, some fluctuation in income may be ignored because of the cushion provided by universal Old Age Security payments. If GIS were the sole means of support fluctuations would pose more serious problems.

Second, the argument that other programs using GIS testing techniques will also be non-stigmatizing implicity defines stigma as a compliance cost rather than the setting apart of an individual from the rest of the community. The method of collecting benefits is simple and relatively painless in the GIS, but the absence of a stigma may as well be a result of the population served in the program. Poverty among the elderly is not seen as the fault of the individual, and the elderly are not generally expected to have employment as their main source of income. Among social assistance recipients on the other hand, if we imagine plushly carpeted social assistance offices with soft lighting and helpful social workers eager to please, a stigmatizing process of self and social identification may nevertheless occur. This is most probable if there is general agreement by society that the receipt of social assistance is indicative of personal failure.

There are also net beneficiaries and net payers in a universal program but initially everyone receives a transfer payment. If the stigma is purely a result of a person's own realization that he or she is a net beneficiary, then there may also be a stigma associated with universal programs. In fact, it is then an unavoidable side-effect of any redistribution. However, this appears most unlikely. First, where the incremental burden and the transfer payment are separated, as in any universal program, it is very difficult to know whether one is a net beneficiary. Second, there does not seem to be any negative connotation to the implicit income test under a universal program, since there is no stigma as a result of failing to bear one's share of the burden.

Two conditions appear necessary and sufficient for a program to be stigmatizing. First, it must be possible to know who is a net beneficiary; and second, there must be a negative connotation to meeting the conditions for eligibility in the program. Demogrants will then be non-stigmatizing because it is not possible to know who is a net beneficiary and there is no negative connotation to membership in a particular demographic group. In a selective program most persons who receive a payment are also net beneficiaries so it is possible for at least the individuals receiving the cheque to know their status. For most non-elderly groups poverty is seen as a sign of failure. Therefore, most selective programs will meet the conditions for stigma.[19]

Whether a social insurance program is stigmatizing will depend upon the 'risk' that is covered as well as the perception of prior contributions. If the event that is insured against is not seen as 'negative,' then the program will probably be non-stigmatizing; for example, the Canada Pension Plan insures for retirement. On the other hand since unemployment may be considered a sign of personal failure, there is usually stigma attached to Unemployment Insurance. But if one has worked for many years and contributed a great deal to UI, then the stigma of collecting upon unemployment may be lessened; one remains a net contributor rather than a net beneficiary.

In general, increased selectivity of either demogrants or social insurance programs will probably increase the stigma associated with the receipt of benefits. Benefits will be viewed as a sign of poverty and personal failure. A general negative income tax (NIT) to replace social insurance and universal programs would also be likely to increase stigma. This is confirmed in a survey conducted in the United States. It was found that their Social Security program had very little or no stigma associated with it, but most respondents felt that there would be a stigma to receiving benefits from an NIT. The study concludes that the 'policy implication is clear. To minimize the social stigma, a program should be designed for all segments of the population' (Williamson 1974, 236).

Reducing stigma
In the preceding discussion, stigma has been distinguished from compliance costs. To be stigmatized is to change as an individual – either in one's own perception or in that of others. It is to be seen as a loser. It results when net

---

19 Where the stigma is reduced, this is probably because the two conditions are not fully met. For example, the Child Tax Credit is generally non-stigmatizing – transfers go to families with fairly high income so it does not indicate poverty, and one's tax contribution may be greater than one's benefit.

beneficiaries can be identified and when eligibility conditions carry negative social connotations. Given these assumptions, selective programs will result in greater stigma than universal programs. But this does not tell us how far we should go in minimizing stigma. It is tempting when discussing stigma to seek to eliminate it rather than to minimize it. But if there is a cost to removing a stigma, at some point we might accept a small amount of stigma if the alternative has large additional costs.

It may seem odd to speak of the 'cost' of stigma. However, a 'shadow price' can be assigned to stigma by finding out how much recipients would be willing to sacrifice to avoid it. Thus for any transfer program in which there is a stigma, there is some lesser amount of money that a recipient would be equally satisfied with if it could be delivered in a completely unstigmatizing fashion. The difference between the two amounts is the price of the stigma, measured according to the preferences of recipients. If we are primarily concerned with the well-being of recipients and if there is a trade-off between stigma and additional costs, then this shadow price will tell us how much to reduce stigma. Any further reduction would be more costly than it would be worth, according to the preferences of the recipients themselves.

Arguments that selective programs divide society and reduce its cohesion run parallel to the discussion of stigma. If programs pay only the poor, then society will be divided into two camps: the people who pay and the people who receive, each resenting the other. On the other hand, since universal programs appear to treat everyone equally, they are viewed as increasing the 'sense of community.' If the sense of community is of value and if it is diminished by selectivity, then this is an added argument in favour of universality.

Of course, this view assumes there is a trade-off with transfer costs. If, instead, stigma, or social non-integration, is just an inefficiency that could be removed by a better design, then no amount is justified. In the past, transfer payments have been treated as a cost. But the previous chapters have argued that transfers are not a cost in any ordinary sense. For example, if to avoid stigma transfers are paid to those with higher incomes but income taxes are increased to pay for the transfers, then there is no real change in private income or the size of government. In many cases selective programs can be duplicated in their redistributive effects by a demogrant. But because there is no stigma attached to tax, there is little or no stigma associated with demogrant programs. Thus, in many cases it appears that there is no real trade-off between a stigma and additional costs; stigma is then simply an inefficiency.

In summary, the necessary and sufficient conditions for stigma appear to be knowledge of who is a net beneficiary and a negative connotation to eligibility. These conditions are more likely to be found in a selective program than in a demogrant. They may or may not occur in a social insurance program depending on the risk that is insured against. But even in the case of social insurance, further increases in selectivity will probably increase the stigma of benefits simply because of the negative social attitude towards poverty. If it is costly to diminish stigma, there is an optimal solution where the costs of stigma (and social non-integration) are equal to the costs of its removal. But in some cases there is no cost; it is just a question of designing programs better and eliminating stigma altogether. In other words, since non-selective programs will usually have less stigma associated with them than selective programs, the problem of stigma as well as the associated values of social integration and cohesion favours universal programs.

FEDERAL-PROVINCIAL RELATIONS

Our federal system demands continuous balancing of the central government's powers with those of the provinces. Income security has traditionally been in the front line of this process for at least two reasons. First, provision for income security under the British North America Act was either unworkable or non-existent and therefore the division of responsibility must be settled politically rather than judicially. Second, the level of government seen as responsible for basic economic security will probably be identified as the level ultimately representative of its citizens. As a result, reform is as likely to succeed or fail according to its impact on federal-provincial relations as on the merits of the reform itself. This section discusses the effect of greater or lesser selectivity on the intergovernmental status quo.

Workers' compensation schemes were the first large-scale income security programs in Canada. Although the BNA Act was silent on income security, except to assign charities to the provinces, the courts ruled that workers' compensation was under provincial jurisdiction. This was not because it was seen as charity; rather, the social insurance scheme was interpreted to be a matter of property and civil rights (Trudeau 1970, 22). The courts have generally defined a program as a social insurance scheme if there are compulsory earmarked contributions, although it is not clear how they would regard a program where the transfers paid were unrelated to the contributions (Bryden 1974, 123–4).

This assignment of responsibilities raised a three-sided problem. According to the BNA Act there would have to be ten compensation schemes, ten contributory pension plans, and ten unemployment insurance programs. But such an arrangement certainly does not appear very efficient or even very possible. An alternative, which would require constitutional amendment, would be a national program in each case. But this might be viewed in Quebec as diminishing the integrity of the province as an entity. Thus a third alternative is two programs – one for Quebec and one for the rest of Canada. But this means that Quebec will have de facto 'special status' among the provinces. The difficulty is then to choose between ten, one, or two programs. None of these choices is without serious problems.

Canada has pragmatically adapted to this problem by trying a different option for each of its three principal social insurance plans. Each province maintains its own workers' compensation program. In 1940 a constitutional amendment gave the Parliament of Canada exclusive jurisdiction over unemployment insurance. In 1951 and 1964 Canada was given the right to legislate with respect to old age and supplementary pension benefits, but the provinces retained paramount jurisdiction in this field since the amendment stated that no law made by Canada respecting old age pensions 'shall affect the operation of any law present or future of a provincial legislature in relation to any such matter' (Section 94A, British North America Act). The result in 1966 was the Quebec Pension Plan in Quebec and the Canada Pension Plan elsewhere.

With respect to social insurance programs, there is at least a constitutional division of powers, although it is not consistent. For other types of income transfer programs there is not even that. The constitutional right of the federal government to run demogrant programs is not clear. There was one legal test of the Family Allowance (FA) program, and the court ruled that the federal parliament could run the program because of 'its power to legislate for peace, order and good government of Canada' (Trudeau 1970, 30). It may also be argued that the program is allowed because of the federal government's 'spending power,' that is, the right of the Parliament of Canada to dispose of its crown assets, including the consolidated fund, as it sees fit. Although constitutional authority for the Old Age Security (OAS) program would seem to be provided on the same basis as the FA, when introducing OAS the federal government apparently felt that specific authority was required. This was the purpose of the 1951 amendment to the BNA Act. The courts may have interpreted the OAS as a pension scheme because a special 'ear-marked' tax was used to fund it. The fund for the OAS was later abolished, but the constitutional amendment remained.

Legal responsibility for selective programs remains equally if not more undecided. The federal constitutional authority for the GIS has not been tested in the courts, but it might be argued to reside in the 1951 and 1964 amendments. It would certainly be difficult to question the right of the federal government to pay tax credits so long as they remain an integral part of the tax system, but matters become less certain as credits become further removed from the tax system. The right of the federal government to run a general income supplement or assistance program remains unclear. Unless these programs were construed as charities under provincial jurisdiction, it is difficult to see how the BNA Act could be interpreted as anything other than silent on the question of jurisdiction over selective programs.

Regardless of the legal division of responsibilities, in practice the federal government's involvement in selective programs has remained limited. Other than the Guaranteed Income Supplement, it did not operate programs providing selective payments except in the limited areas of native and veterans' benefits. Federal involvement was restricted to social insurance, demogrants, and cost-sharing of provincial programs. Provincial governments made selective payments, usually cost-shared, as part of their social assistance programs. Recently, in addition to the GIS, the federal government has introduced another major selective program, the Refundable Child Tax Credit (RCTC). This leaves odd contradictions between jurisdictional authority and the actual operation of the programs. The result is not always consistent and certainly does not follow any evidently rational pattern. Table 8 summarizes the existing legal and actual authority for income security programs in Canada.

The three most likely programs for increased selectivity are all federal: FA, OAS, and Unemployment Insurance. The RCTC probably brought the income tax system close to its limits as a means of delivering transfers. Any program providing much larger average benefits would have to be paid more often than once a year, test income on a more current basis than the preceding tax year, and probably require a more refined definition of income. This is essentially the point made in Canada (1978). Thus further 'conversion' of the FA into a selective program will probably require a new administrative mechanism at least one step removed from the tax system. As discussed above, the constitutional authority for such a program is not evident.

Similarly, if UI is increasingly income-tested it would seem to lose the characteristics of insurance, at least as it has been interpreted by the courts. This is because the connection between contributions and benefits would be reduced. As such it is difficult to see how it could fall under the provisions of the 1940 amendment to the BNA Act. Thus, of the three main candidates for change, only the OAS appears to present no *new* constitutional questions, since the OAS would probably be made more selective through the already existing GIS. This is not to say that the GIS is not without its own constitutional ambiguities.

TABLE 8
Legal and actual responsibility for major income security programs, 1980

Program	Legal responsibility	Actual responsibility
Demogrants		
Family allowance	Co-jurisdictional	Mainly federal government with provinces allowed to vary payment according to federal criteria. Quebec has own family allowance to supplement federal. PEI had program, now cancelled.
Old Age Security	Co-jurisdictional*	Only the federal government pays demogrants to the elderly.
Social Insurance		
Pensions	Co-jurisdictional for public pensions with provincial paramountcy	Canada Pension Plan operative everywhere but in Quebec, administered by federal government; change requires consent of ⅔ of provinces with ⅔ of population. Quebec runs its own public pension plan.
Unemployment Insurance	Federal government	Federal government: sometimes consultation will be sought with provinces before a program change.
Workers' compensation	Provinces	Provinces: loose co-ordination is maintained voluntarily by provinces.
Veterans' benefits	Federal government	Federal government (some veterans' benefits are income tested).
Selective programs		
Income-tested benefits for the elderly	Co-jurisdictional*	Federal government with 'top-up' programs in six provinces and shelter allowance in three
Income-tested child benefits	Co-jurisdictional*	Federal government pays annual child tax credit: two provinces have income tested monthly programs aside from social assistance. Some influence by federal government on provincial programs through cost sharing.
Social Assistance	Co-jurisdictional*	Provinces only but large federal impact through cost sharing
Income supplements and tax credits	Co-jurisdictional*	Only one province now has plans for a supplement not related to children; a few provinces now have extensive tax credit plans that function as an income supplement.

* Signifies a judicially untested or unclear assignment of legal responsibility.

Through its spending power or through the peace, order and good government provision, the federal government *may* be legally competent to deliver more selective benefits. Regardless of the legal position, its direct participation in paying those in need could be viewed as an encroachment on traditional provincial responsibility. Taking a longer-range view, general income supplementation is bound to develop in a modern industrialized state such as Canada. At present the provinces are beginning to fill this role, allbeit in a tentative and perhaps less than fully satisfactory manner. The level of government that delivers supplementation will increase its relative importance in the life of the nation. This point is reflected in the white paper on Quebec's referendum: 'by creating a supplementary income plan in 1979, the Quebec government has shown to what extent it is determined to ... harmonize former federal programs with programs already managed in Quebec so as to create a coherent system of income security' (Quebec 1979). The authors of the white paper see Quebec's right to assert its sovereignty as demonstrated by its ability to provide comprehensive income security, particularly when contrasted with the apparent inability of the federal government.

Two intergovernmental issues emerge with respect to increased selectivity. First, does such an approach require a change in the de jure powers of the federal government? Second, does increased selectivity imply a de facto shift in the relative powers of the levels of government? Of course an alternative to increasing the selectivity of existing programs under the present administrative arrangements is for the federal government to hand over revenues to the provinces or enter into further cost-sharing arrangements so that provinces would run new selective programs. This avoids the problem of de jure division of responsibility, but it certainly does not avoid a de facto shift of power to the provinces. The decision as to which level of government ought ultimately to be responsible for a given type of program goes beyond the scope of this study. Yet, whatever the decision, the intergovernmental implications of the universality–selectivity debate must be noted.

Aside from the problems of constitutional jurisdiction and changes in the relative importance of federal services, increased selectivity may also make integration and co-ordination of income security programs more difficult. For example, when the Refundable Child Tax Credit was introduced, Family Allowance payments were simultaneously lowered from approximately $25 to $20. This meant less *monthly* income for families with children. Of course, this was more than compensated for by the new tax credit. But the tax credit was delivered on a *yearly* basis. Most families could easily afford to budget their tax credit through the year. Families on provincial social assistance do not, however, have monthly budgets large enough to allow this leeway. Benefits at the beginning or the end of the year do little for needs in the middle of the year. But if provinces attempted to replace the lost monthly Family Allowance, this would entail a large unplanned increase in provincial expenditures as well as a double bonus for assistance recipients compared to others. If the province attempted to collect the extra bonus when the Child Tax Credit was paid at the end of the year, it would undoubtedly be accused of negating the federal program and taking money from the poor.

Not all changes in federal programs will affect the provinces in precisely this way, but greater selectivity will usually cause increased problems of co-ordination and integration with social assistance and other programs. In general, transfers paid in a universal program are easier to plan for within a program providing selective benefits. It is exceptionally difficult for two selective programs to complement each other. Except for a brief comment by Kapsalis (1980), this aspect of the universality–selectivity debate has been virtually ignored.

Federal–provincial relations have rarely been mentioned in economists' discussions of income security reform in Canada. Yet income security reform and federal–provincial relations are intimately connected. This is dramatically substantiated in accounts of the Victoria Charter's demise (Simeon 1972, Smiley 1972) as well as in accounts of the Federal–Provincial Social Security Review (Van Loon 1979). Increased difficulty and complexity of federal–provincial relations is a price to be paid for increased selectivity. Whether it is worth paying depends upon one's assessment of the benefits of greater selectivity.

5
Universal and selective alternatives

Three programs in Canada's income security system have been selectivists' favourite targets for reform: Family Allowance, Old Age Security, and Unemployment Insurance. This chapter analyses some proposals that have been made for turning these programs into selective plans.

FAMILY ALLOWANCE

A common proposal for greater selectivity of Family Allowance (FA) is to use a reduction in FA transfers to finance a selective program of child-related benefits. This approach has a long history in Canada, going back at least to the Family Income Security Plan (FISP) proposed in the white paper of 1970 (Canada 1970). The FISP would have increased maximum payments for those with low incomes, but transfers would have gradually diminished to zero as income increased.

The FISP was supported by the provinces but not by the opposition parties or many of the general public. The FISP Bill was not passed by Parliament and by late 1973 it was all but forgotten. In January, 1974 the FA was instead *increased* to $20 per month per child and was made taxable, to be treated the same way for income tax purposes as most other forms of income. This signalled the whole-hearted adoption of a universalist approach. The reversal of earlier selectivist policies was largely unmentioned; nor did discussion of the 1974 changes address the selectivist alternative.

By 1978 the universalism of 1974 was ripe for another reversal. Since the FA had been indexed to the cost of living, rapid inflation meant that its nominal flow through the federal treasury had increased substantially. There was intense pressure on the federal government to decrease spending in the hope that this might somehow reduce inflation. The federal government responded by reducing negative taxes through a decrease in FA, rather than changing its spending on goods and services. The tax increase was offset by a new tax credit, the Refundable Child Tax Credit (RCTC). Since the tax credit is treated as a revenue reduction rather than an increase in spending, the result is to show a reduction in government expenditures, without any real change.

The RCTC was based on 1978 income, but was paid in 1979 through income tax refunds or as a reduction on tax payable. It paid a maximum of $200 per child to those with less than $18,000 taxable family income, with a 5 per cent rate of reduction as income increased. The RCTC was financed primarily by a $5.68 per child per month reduction in FA. It was also paid for by a decrease in the income tax exemption for children aged sixteen to seventeen and the cancellation of a $50 non-refundable tax credit per child.

Because the RCTC was financed from a number of sources it is difficult to measure its distributional implications precisely. An accurate calculation of winners and losers from various child-related benefit plans would require the review of a large sample of micro-data on individuals and their families. Although that empirical exercise is beyond the scope of this study, it is possible to use averages within each income class to illustrate potential distributive consequences of alternative plans. Table 9 shows some of these possible outcomes. The distributive consequence of the RCTC is illustrated in column 2, 'pre-1978 to post-1978.' As may be seen, the pattern of net income change is of benefit to the three lowest quintiles at the expense of the two highest. However, it is the fourth rather than the fifth quintile that bears the greatest burden, and it is the third rather than the first or second quintile that derives the greatest benefit.

Accepting the RCTC changes after 1978 as accomplished, what then would be the consequence of now going 'all the way' with a selectivist approach? Column 3 presents a possible outcome of an $800 maximum RCTC per child per year decreasing by 5 per cent on all family income beyond $10,000, coupled with cancellation of the FA. This program would require a small increase in over-all transfers. The net result would be that the fifth quintile bears the brunt of financing the improved benefits for the lowest quintiles and the middle quintile remains hardly affected. Given these preliminary illustrations, it is thus possible that the impact of a more thorough selectivist approach may therefore be a progressive income re-distribution if over-all transfers are increased or not reduced.

An alternative to the selectivist approach is to return to the universalism of before 1978. It was just four years before the RCTC was introduced that the federal government massively increased the universal FA financed from gen-

TABLE 9
Possible distributive effects of various plans for child related benefits
(average dollar change per family in each quintile) [a]

	Net income change		
Quintile	Pre-1978 program [b] post-1978 program [c]	Post-1978 program to $800 RCTC [d]	Post-1978 program to $65 FA [e]
1	52	169	106
2	68	259	75
3	102	49	18
4	−125	−82	150
5	−98	−401	−347

a This table has been calculated for purposes of illustration only, and represents a *possible* distributive outcome of alternative plans. It is calculated as if every family in each quintile had the average family income for the quintile, the average number of children, and the average number of spouses. Tax tables for 1978 were then used to calculate net benefits of various alternatives, and tax shares were assigned on the basis of 1, 7, 16, 25, and 51% for the lowest through the highest quintiles respectively. Figures were reconciled against known aggregates, such as total FA transfers, where possible.

b Pre-1978 program is Family Allowance of $25.68 per child per month, a dependent child income tax exemption of $460 per child under 16 and $840 per child 16+, and a non-refundable child tax credit of $50 per child.

c Post-1978 program is Family Allowance of $20 per child per month, dependent child tax exemption of $460 for all children under 18, and a Refundable Child Tax Credit of maximum $200 per child per year decreasing by 5% for taxable family income above $18,000. (The reduction in exemptions for children between 16 and 18 was actually phased in over two years).

d RCTC maximum of $800 per child per year decreasing by 5% of taxable family income above $10,000, no FA, child exemption of $460 per child under 18.

e $65 Family Allowance per child per month, no RCTC, child exemption of $460 per child under 18.

eral revenue. A cynic might suggest that federal policy with respect to FA has operated on a four-year cycle, and that a return to universalist policies could be expected in 1982. The purest universalist policy is simply to increase FA as was done in 1974. This would also result in a progressive redistribution of income, as is illustrated in column 4 of Table 9. This column shows the possible distributive impact of increasing the FA demogrant to $65 per month per child and cancelling the RCTC. Of course, it should be emphasized once more that these results are dependent upon the assumptions made about distribution of tax changes.

There are also other, less pure universalist policies. A 'quasi-universalist' approach that has received much consideration is to increase the family allowance but impose a surtax on higher incomes. One of the first recommendations to increase FA along with a surtax was made by Quebec's 'Report of the Commission of Inquiry on Health and Social Welfare,' popularly known as the Castonguay-Nepveu report. It recommended 'recuperating a fraction of family allowances through income tax by means of a distinct scale of taxation of family allowance' (Quebec 1971, 136). Families with higher incomes would have to reimburse their family allowance fully. Similar proposals have also surfaced more recently. For example, Bergeron (1979) sees two alternatives: 'Family Allowances could be recovered completely from families above the $26,000 point at which the child tax credit program now phases out. Alternatively, family allowances could be recovered completely from those earning above average family income, which is now just over $21,000 per year' (ibid., 75). Bergeron does not explain why he mentions only these two options. Kapsalis (1980) also attempts to defend family allowance by pursuing a similar 'tax back' route.

These proposals would result in an income distribution similar to those for selective and purer universal approaches. One difference is that the size of government spending as traditionally recorded would increase compared to the selective alternative. There may also be differences with respect to administration and institutional arrangements: these are discussed below. So far as distribution is concerned it is difficult to shake the suspicion that advocates of tax reimbursement have simply forgotten that if the tax system is progressive (or even mildly regressive) those with high incomes are already paying more than they are receiving. If, on the other hand, the tax system is insufficiently progressive, then should FA or other forms of transfer income be singled out for special attention in attempting to correct this fault in the tax system?

What all this means is that if one were concerned only about progressivity, either a RCTC replacing FA, an increased FA accompanied by a tax surcharge, or an increased FA financed from general revenue would probably be equally acceptable. But a tax transfer change is not necessarily desirable just because it is progressive, even from a purely distributional view. Although programs to redistribute between income classes will probably be judged by whether they are progressive, not all programs need have redistribution between income classes as their objective. Some programs will have to redistribute *within* income classes if horizontal equity is to be achieved.

As shown in Table 4, few of those in lower income groups have children, so that a program providing child-related benefits will have only limited success in redistribution to lower income groups no matter how selective it is. Most of the poor remain excluded just because they do not have children. Programs providing child-related benefits are therefore not very effective anti-poverty mechanisms. Child-related benefits are usually rationalized on the grounds that 'income from employment or from social insurance does not ordinarily take account of family size' (Canada 1973, 18). Thus families with low incomes need assistance to raise children. But after differences in need are taken into account, families of low income without children may also require assistance because they are in poverty. It would seem more logical to provide net benefits on the basis of poverty if the goal is to provide assistance to the poor. Programs providing child-related benefits may therefore be more suitable for redistribution within income groups rather than between income groups.

Apart from distributional consequences there are likely to be important administrative differences in the different approaches to FA. The most important administrative problem associated with the RCTC and further selectivist reform is an inability to provide benefits that are responsive to changes in income at the time that the changes occur. The RCTC is based on last year's income and is paid in one lump sum when income tax refunds are made. But for poor families, it may be extraordinarily difficult to budget a single payment through the whole year.

This problem could be slightly ameliorated if RCTC payments were made more frequently than once yearly. Imagine for example, that the RCTC was paid quarterly rather than annually. As long as a family's income remained constant from one year to the next, transfers would be commensurate with needs. But if income changed suddenly, the RCTC would be of no help. As long as RCTC payments are relatively small, lack of responsiveness is not of paramount importance. Since the payments are too small to be a major source of income, rather than providing basic necessities on a daily basis they are instead a kind of 'bonus.' But if the RCTC becomes much larger and replaces other programs it will be a means of subsistence for very poor families. A cheque not issued when need arose would then have serious consequences. Given the current method of administration the RCTC is thus limited in size.

Participation rates are another administrative problem for the RCTC. Unfortunately, there are no reliable data and no published studies indicating the percentage of those eligible for the RCTC who have actually received it. No doubt, as the use of the income tax for purposes of delivering a credit increases, more persons will file income tax returns and receive the credits to which they are entitled. But it is difficult to see why the participation rate for the RCTC should ever be expected to exceed the rates for the GIS. As noted in Chapter 2, GIS participation rates are about 85 per cent according to the best estimate available. Since the amounts involved for the RCTC are usually much smaller than the GIS, and the public is generally less aware of the newer program, it is likely that RCTC rates are now less than those for the GIS.

The RCTC also presents special institutional problems in Canada's complex income security system. The FA may be readily co-ordinated with other programs because it pays an amount that is either uniform or, in some provinces, adjusted according to easily ascertained criteria such as age of the children. This means that programs like Social Assistance and Unemployment Insurance can readily adjust their benefits to take account of the availability of FA. But the RCTC presents much more difficulty. As long as the RCTC is paid annually, social assistance programs will be confronted with an insoluble dilemma – 'continuing to set social assistance levels on a monthly basis will mean higher than intended standards of adequacy on an annual basis, while setting those levels on an annual basis may result in hardship in any month' (Interprovincial Task Force on Social Security 1980, 111). Even if the RCTC were paid more often than annually, other programs would then face the added administrative problem of finding out what the RCTC is in a given month, verifying the reports, and adjusting their payments.

As important as these administrative problems is the de facto expansion of the federal government into what has traditionally been a provincial domain. If the federal government increased the RCTC enough that it became a major source of income for low-income families, designed to ensure that basic necessities could be provided, this would be an encroachment on provincial responsibility. This may or may not be desirable, but it certainly adds to the strains on our federal system.

In summary, the distributional effects of increased selectivity in the family allowance, whether accomplished by decreasing FA in favour of the RCTC or some other mechanism, may be duplicated by either universalist or quasi-universalist approaches. On the other hand, there are a number of administrative and institutional disadvantages to increasing the selectivity of the FA, particularly if it is accomplished through the RCTC. The RCTC is not responsive to changes in income and it will not have participation rates as high as those for the universalist approaches. It will also be difficult to integrate into the social security system and may disrupt the existing intergovernmental status quo. The only advantage for the RCTC is the *illusion* of reducing federal spending. This is a dubious advantage.

OLD AGE SECURITY

Old Age Security (OAS) is Canada's largest demogrant program, paying each person 65 and over about $2400 annually (1980). Since 1966 all OAS recipients have also been eligible for the Guaranteed Income Supplement (GIS). The GIS is a selective program with a maximum payment about equal to the OAS, but reduced by $1 for every $2 of a recipient's income (measured retrospectively through the income tax system). There have been several proposals to reduce the OAS in favour of the GIS. The existence of an already functioning administration for the selective GIS has no doubt made such policies more attractive.

The federal white paper, *Income Security for Canadians* (Canada 1970), argued strongly against reductions in the OAS. According to the white paper, to get rid of the flat rate OAS 'would be inappropriate since benefit provisions for the Canada and Quebec Pension Plans were developed on the basis that this flat rate pension would be there as a foundation. To withdraw it now would force a reconsideration of retirement benefits under those Plans. Many people have planned their retirement on the expectation that they will get Old Age Security at age 65, and to deny them this benefit would be extremely unfair and a breach of faith. Personal income taxes as well as other earmarked taxes have been collected from people since 1952 to finance this program, establishing an expectation and a right to the pension. Under these circumstances, action to restrict the program's universality would be difficult to justify' (Canada 1970, 69).

Surprisingly, the white paper then went on to contradict itself by recommending that further increases, which would have gone into the OAS to keep up with inflation, should instead go into the GIS. This was almost the only recommendation of the white paper to find its way into legislation. Effective 1 January 1971 the OAS was set at $80 and further cost of living increases calculated on the basis of the combined OAS/GIS were to be added to the GIS alone. There is no substantive difference between reducing OAS in one year by legislation or letting the real value of the OAS be diminished over several years by inflation. If the white paper's authors had read their own arguments more carefully, they might have been able to predict the hostile reaction to this innovation. Having adopted the policy that it argued against, the White Paper legislation was reversed effective 1 January 1971, and the basic OAS was fully indexed to the cost of living.

Ten years later, the Economic Council of Canada, in its report *One in Three* (1979), took precisely the reverse strategy. It seemed to argue that the OAS should be discontinued in favour of the GIS, but it then recommended that 'all payments under the OAS and GIS programs continue to be indexed to the consumer price index' (ECC 1979, 100). The ECC's main argument in favour of the GIS was that reducing the OAS 'would offer a way to reduce expenditures or to raise the basic pension for those most in need without raising costs' (EEC 1979, 90). The ECC recognized that there had been several disadvantages to income-tested programs in the past, including 'stigma,' but felt that techniques available today, namely use of the income tax system, would allow a means-tested program to avoid those problems.

As has been discussed in earlier chapters, the supposed benefits of increased selectivity, cost-saving, and possible distributional advantages do not stand up to closer scrutiny. The 'cost-saving' is the same as would be gained by an increase in taxes and does not constitute any reduction in government spending on goods and services. The distributional advantages are present only if benefits are counted but costs are excluded – the distribution of net benefits for a universal program may be just as progressive as those for a selective program. Furthermore, the distributional effects of a change in policy cannot be described solely by the pattern of new benefits. It is the *difference* between the new and the old that entails a change in income.

Table 10 illustrates a possible net change in income that might result from either a complete selectivist or a complete universalist alternative. Both alternatives provide the same maximum payment to those with no income in the current system, but in the selective alternative it would all be paid through the GIS, while in the universal alternative it would all be paid through the OAS. The former program entails a decrease of about $1 billion in the flow of transfers through government, while the latter program requires an increase of about $1.2 billion. Since the average benefit in each quintile will vary greatly depending upon whether a family unit happens to include someone over 65, net income changes on Table 10 are broken down between beneficiaries and non-beneficiaries. As may be seen, making the OAS completely selective amounts mainly to a tax on the elderly in middle and upper quintiles. On the other hand, the main beneficiaries of the universal alternative would be the lower-middle and higher quintiles among the elderly at the expense of higher-income groups among the non-elderly. While neither of these alternatives has precisely the desired distributional effects that their advocates might claim, the universalist approach at least transfers from those under 65 to those over, rather than the reverse.

Leaving aside distributional questions, the administrative problems of simply adding the OAS to the GIS may be somewhat larger than expected. Again the problem is one of responsiveness. As long as the universal OAS continues to pay substantial amounts each month regardless of changes in

TABLE 10
Possible distributive effects of alternative transfer programs for the elderly
(average dollar change per family unit in each quintile)

Quintiie	Net income change from making OAS selective and adding it to the GIS		Net income change from making GIS universal and adding it to the OAS	
	Beneficiary	Non-beneficiary	Beneficiary	Non-beneficiary
1	0	0	0	0
2	−806	40	1865	−47
3	−2878	108	1788	−124
4	−2826	160	1725	−187
5	−2624	362	1492	−420

NOTE: Using OAS rate of $1938 and GIS rate of $1369 and $1188 for a single or married recipient respectively: approximating rates in 1978. This table has been calculated for illustration only and represents a possible distributive outcome of alternative plans. It is calculated as if every family were of average size. This means that elderly families have 0.54 of a spouse. Tax tables for 1978 were used to calculate net benefits of various alternatives, and tax shares were assigned on the basis of 1 per cent, 16 per cent, 25 per cent, and 51 per cent for the lowest through the highest quintiles respectively. Figures were reconciled against known aggregates where possible. The total flow of transfers through the federal government would be reduced by about a billion dollars by the selectivist alternative. This agrees with estimates in ECC (1979). The universal alternative would increase the flow of transfers by about $1.2 billion.

An accurate calculation of net benefits would require the review of a large sample of micro data, and is beyond the scope of this paper. This table illustrates that those who gain most from a selectivist alternative *may* be the wealthy non-elderly.

income, the GIS lack of responsiveness to changes in income may be tolerable. But if there were no universal pension it would be difficult to base all payments on last year's taxable income without causing extraordinary hardship. The administrative ease of the GIS is often thought to demonstrate that a selective program is workable. It may instead demonstrate that a selective program is workable only if it is complemented by a universal program.

UNEMPLOYMENT INSURANCE

Unlike the other programs discussed in this chapter, Unemployment Insurance does not pay a flat amount to everyone in a broad demographic category. Rather, the payments depend on previous contributions and upon the recipient's availability for employment. Nevertheless, UI is 'universal' as that term has been defined here because the payments are not related to income or wealth. Whether applicants for UI have a private income of a million dollars a year or none at all, they may still be eligible for UI.

Although there may be a few cases where an Unemployment Insurance recipient really does have a sizable private income, this is probably the least common case of payments going to those who are not poor. It is much more likely that income over a whole year will be sizable because the term of unemployment will be short. For example, if Mr Jones has a job for $25,000 a year and is laid off for four weeks, his annual income will still be about $23,000. Thus, while many of those collecting UI may have low income receipts when they are on UI, their income over the year may in any event be substantial. Another time when UI often goes to a family whose income is not low is when a family has two earners only one of whom is unemployed. For example, if Mr and Mrs Jones both earn $25,000 annually and Mr Jones is laid off, the family will still have a substantial income.

It would therefore be foolish to suggest a straightforward selectivist policy of income-testing UI recipients at the time of payment, because unemployment is most likely to coincide with at least a temporary cash flow deficiency for the individual. The main recommendations for greater selectivity in the UI are thus to enlarge the accounting period to a full year so that UI would be income-tested annually through the tax system, and to use family income and family unemployment to determine eligibility.

One family-based approach analysed by Cloutier and Smith (1980) is to make the family the basic insurable unit and to grant UI payments only when *family* income fell below the family's total insurable earnings as a result of unemployment. For example, say Mr and Mrs Jones were each working at an annual salary of $25,000 and each had insurable earnings of $12,000. If Mr Jones became unemployed, he would not be entitled to any UI because the family's earnings would remain more than the family's insurable earnings. In other words, as long as one spouse was earning more than the family's insurable earnings, the second spouse would be effectively disentitled to UI. If the family's earnings fell below their total insurable level, UI would pay 60 per cent (the current standard rate) of the difference.

The Cloutier–Smith proposal is clearly not a true selectivist approach. There would still be no income-testing of UI payments; rather UI would ensure against a decrease in income caused by unemployment of a family unit. Thus an individual with high income would collect benefits if unemployed for two months, but a couple who together had the same high income would not collect benefits even if one of them was unemployed for several months. According to Cloutier and Smith the distribution of benefits would be more progressive if UI were provided on a family instead of an individual basis. But it is not self-evident that the distribution of *net* changes in income would also be progressive. This will depend upon whether losses in transfers would be offset by reductions in taxes. Cloutier and Smith do not calculate the distribution of tax reductions, and, as discussed in Chapter 2, they therefore fail to trace 'all the gains and losses' resulting from a family based approach.

Table 11 presents a possible distribution of net benefits for a family-based UI on the assumption that all tax changes will be made in income tax rather than the payroll tax.[20] If the family-based UI resulted in a 10 per cent decrease in over-all transfers, then the distribution of average net change in income would be primarily in favour of the second and third quintiles and would be paid for almost entirely by the fifth quintile. The average net change for any income group is very small. Redistribution from the fifth to the third quintile is not of much benefit to the lowest-income quintile. This is based on the most progressive family-based scheme; other plans would have a similar but less dramatic pattern of net benefit distribution. The Cloutier–Smith plan would also undermine the justification for the current system of contributions based on individual earnings.

Osberg (1979) has suggested a quasi-universalist alternative also treating the family unit as a whole, but using the income tax system to place a surtax on a family's Unemployment Insurance transfers. The surtax would be calculated according to total family income rather than individual income and would be based on the family's annual income rather than their income at the time of unemployment. But the average net change in income for each quintile would be progressive only if the tax rates on the surcharge were more progressive than the compensating reduction in other taxes.

Both the Cloutier–Smith and the Osberg proposals would reduce the net income of those who are unemployed and increase the net income of those who do not experience unemployment (although this increase in income might be largely confined to upper incomes). The Osberg proposal would increase government revenue by placing a tax on the unemployed; the Cloutier–Smith proposal would decrease government 'costs' by reducing transfers to the unemployed. Neither proposal would decrease government spending on goods and services. Both proposals are essentially ways to increase tax revenue, either through increasing positive taxes or decreasing

20 Table 11 has been calculated primarily according to Cloutier and Smith's results, but it should be treated as only broadly indicative of a potential net result since it is simply based on their summary data rather than an analysis of a sample of individuals.

TABLE 11

Possible distributive effects of a family-based unemployment insurance
(average dollar change per family in each quintile)

Income quintile	Assuming 10% reduction in transfers		
	$ change in transfers[a]	$ change in tax[b]	Net change in income ($)
1	0	0	0
2	0	+10.31	+10.31
3	−6.19	+35.06	+28.87
4	−63.94	+57.75	−6.19
5	−136.13	+103.13	−33.00

a Assuming that for quintiles 1, 2, 3, 4, and 5 respectively the distribution of
transfers was 8.1, 22, 25, 22.6 and 22.3%. These are the estimates derived
by Cloutier (1978) for UI in 1975. Also assuming that the first and second
quintiles have no reduction in transfers as a result of the family based plan,
that the third quintile has 3% of total reductions, the fourth 31% of total
reductions, and the fifth 66% of total reductions. These are the shares of
total reductions estimated by Cloutier and Smith (1980) for their most
progressive family based scheme (p. 38). Further assume 1.6 million units
in each quintile and total transfers of $3.3 billion before the introduction of
the family based scheme.

b Tax changes are calculated assuming that only income tax financing will be
reduced, and that payroll contributions will remain as is. Tax cuts are
therefore apportioned to quintiles 1, 2, 3, 4, and 5 respectively as follows:
0, 5, 17, 23, and 50%. These are approximately Cloutier's estimates of the
direct financing burden for Family Allowance (Cloutier, 1978; see also
Table 2 above).

negative taxes for the unemployed. It may be that the federal government
needs increased tax revenue and that this is a laudable national objective.
However, it is not clear why the unemployed should be singled out to bear a
disproportionate burden of meeting this objective. An increase in ability-to-
pay taxes, with the employed wealthy also bearing their fair share, would
seem a more logical and equitable method of raising tax revenue.

Since the dispersion of benefits within income groups may be more important than the distribution between groups, is it useful to view UI as a means
for distribution between income groups? Unemployment occurs within all
income groups and is not necessarily concentrated among those with least
income. Therefore, paying transfers when unemployment occurs is not likely
to redistribute to those with the lowest income. It will instead distribute to

those who are unemployed. For example, UI could be made more progressive if it were financed entirely by income tax rather than from the payroll tax. But the net beneficiaries would remain the officially unemployed among all or almost all income classes. Those who are poor and had not been part of the labour force would gain very little if at all from such changes. The conclusion is that UI is not very good at redistributing income. But then what is unemployment insurance good for?

One simple reason for UI is to insure against loss of income due to unemployment. Since loss of income is not confined to those with low incomes, particularly over the whole year or when family resources are taken into account, such an insurance would not necessarily redistribute income between income groups. Many commentators have, however, found great difficulty in regarding UI as an insurance. This is apparently because it is believed that private insurance requires differential contribution rates according to risk groups. By this definition the malpractice insurance offered by the Ontario Medical Association or the Auto Workers' dental plan cannot be considered insurance. In fact, group insurance does not require different contributions according to risk.

The *economic* argument for unemployment insurance is not, however, based on whether it resembles private insurance. Rather, as discussed in Chapter 2, it is based on the notion of declining marginal utility of income. This means that the more income one has, the less benefit one gets from each additional, or marginal, dollar. As long as this is true, people are better off in a world where there is unemployment insurance than a world where there is none, so that by making contributions they may 'transfer' income from a time when they have more money to a time when they have less.

In economic terms, the availability of insurance is a question of efficiency, not equity. Except possibly for extremely high (and maybe extremely low) incomes, where the marginal utility of income may not be decreasing, this applies regardless of the level of income. Whether income is high or low, people will be better off having the opportunity to insure against a risk of losing income. If they are economically rational they will seek ways to purchase such insurance (unless they enjoy the thrill of a risk for its own sake).

This, of course, is only an argument for insurance; it is not an argument for a compulsory and publicly run insurance. The latter may be justified because a private insurance is impossible or socially unacceptable. A private unemployment insurance may be impossible because the risk is completely unpredictable or unmeasurable. Voluntary insurance might not be possible because of adverse selection, where only those who have the highest risk will purchase the insurance. A private insurance may be considered socially undesirable if, for example, it is a monopoly and insurance is compulsory.

It is beyond the scope of this study to consider whether unemployment insurance should be publicly provided. The point here is that there is a perfectly legitimate role for a non-redistributive UI. If redistributive objectives are to be imposed on UI it will be at the risk of failing to obtain other objectives. One might more readily redistribute by increasing programs whose net benefits are distributed according to income rather than to non-income related criteria such as unemployment or number of children.

6
Conclusion

This chapter is a general summary of the policies that may follow from the arguments presented in this study. If considerations of equity, efficiency and institutional arrangements are carefully weighed, what would the resulting 'model' income security system look like?

In this study a set of criteria, or a kind of 'checklist,' has been used to analyse critically the universality–selectivity debate. According to this checklist there are three questions we should ask of any proposal to reform income security programs: Is it fair? Is it efficient? Is it compatable with Canada's social and institutional structure?

Within each of these three broad areas there are a number of specific considerations. Most important, the fairness of a program depends upon the distribution of its net benefits and not just its transfers. It is in this respect that this study differs from many others. Of course, this method of analysis necessitates assumptions about the distribution of tax changes, but the alternative seems to be merely to ignore tax changes. In assessing the fairness of a program, it is also necessary to take account of family size and of income throughout a lifetime as well as in a year or a month. It may be misleading to look only at the average impact of a program in each income group, since the impact may be quite dispersed. For categorical programs the distributive impact may be best analysed by separating recipients form non-recipients. Furthermore, the immediate effect of a transfer program will not be the same as the ultimate incidence when behavioural effects and tax-transfer shifting are taken into account. Finally, not all income security programs necessarily have redistribution to those with low incomes as their primary goal. Some programs may redistribute 'horizontally' within income groups and others may be insurance programs.

In economic terms a program will be 'inefficient' if it reduces the total value of goods and services available including the value of leisure time. Because any tax–transfer system will distort relative prices, there will always be some loss of efficiency. The size of the loss will depend on the amount of distortion, which in turn depends, among other things, upon the response of labour supply and savings. The administrative cost of a program will be an additional burden. Since all programs will to some extent distort relative prices, the key to the efficiency criterion is to minimize inefficiency for a given amount of redistribution or other tax–transfer objective. In practical terms this usually means keeping administrative costs, work disincentives, and savings disincentives as low as possible.

Finally, there are a group of diverse institutional and social factors to be considered in the design of income-transfer programs. Probably most important of all is to minimize or eliminate 'stigma.' In Canada, our sensitive federalist state also demands that tax–transfer systems realistically take account of the federal–provincial arrangements that have evolved over the past century.

Given these criteria, it is possible to describe in general what a model income security system would look like; and it may also be possible to describe what it would *not* look like. A model income security system would consist of several programs to serve a number of different purposes. There would have to be some program to provide income for the poor and redistribute command over resources. But income replacement objectives require other programs that do not redistribute from the rich to the poor. These would instead redistribute from the employed to the unemployed, from the pre-retired to the retired, and from the well to the injured. Horizontal equity demands further redistribution within rather than between income classes.

A model income security system would therefore not consist of a single, monolithic negative income tax (NIT). Since the late 1950s there has been a consensus, shared among scholars of both the right and the left, that the ideal income security reform would be to sweep aside all programs along with their accompanying administrative and regulatory apparatus and replace them with one program – the NIT. In its ideal form it was believed that the NIT would be fully integrated both in terms of tax rates and administration with the positive income tax system. Long and sometimes bitter experience has now convinced most observers of the income security system that such integration is a pipe dream. Nevertheless, the ideal of a single, simple NIT to replace all programs remains dominant.

Obviously, at least one of the programs in the model system must be an anti-poverty device, as the NIT is meant to be, but there is no justification for assuming that the NIT is the best program for this purpose. The NIT is only one of several forms for the guaranteed annual income (GAI). The credit income tax (CIT) is another form of GAI. The CIT would credit everyone a specific amount, although it could pay higher amounts to persons in specific categories. The CIT would also reform the whole personal and corporate income tax system and institute a proportionate tax on all income. The CIT would appear preferable to the NIT according to most of the criteria discussed in this paper. In terms of redistribution and efficiency, aside from administration, the programs are roughly equivalent but in terms of administration, the CIT appears to have several advantages (see Kesselman 1981). Most important, the CIT is less stigmatizing than the NIT.

The CIT has the added advantage of being possible to implement gradually rather than all at once (see Kesselman 1981b). A first step could be to convert the current system of personal tax exemptions to credits, where the size of the credits would be established so that there would be no revenue lost by government. Marginal tax rates could then be flattened out across income groups, so that those with lower incomes would pay higher marginal tax rates and those with higher incomes pay lower marginal rates. This would partially compensate for the redistributive shift in tax burdens resulting from the credit.

Unfortunately, both the NIT and the CIT appear very difficult to institute within Canada's federal–provincial arrangements. The operation of a basic anti-poverty program has traditionally been a function of provincial governments. Even a small CIT would be very difficult to integrate with provincial programs. For those Canadians who are more concerned with the quality of programs, the basic point at issue is whether assistance for the poor in any given province should be the responsibility only of the wealthy in that province, or whether assistance for the poor anywhere in Canada is the responsibility of the wealthy of the whole country. Once this question is answered, the federal–provincial arrangements required to provide a CIT or NIT could more readily be established.

Programs to provide horizontal equity for families with children, for the aged, or for those with handicaps will also be part of a model income security system. The precise instrument for such programs may be either credits within the tax system or demogrants. Finally, social insurance plans are likely to continue in their current prominent role. In fact they might be expanded to provide better compensation for disability, for disease, and for those who are not employed in paid labour.

The evolution of a model income security system is fundamentally impeded by the accounting treatment of transfers as government spending rather than as negative taxes. This problem might be partly solved if the trend continues to rely increasingly upon departments of finance and revenue to plan and deliver income security programs. As a single agency becomes responsible for the whole tax–transfer system, it is likely that the system will begin to be treated in a more homogeneous fashion. If transfers were recorded in the revenue side of budgets (see Mendelson 1981), this might further assist in the development of rational social policy.

The basic objective of proposals to increase selectivity has been to improve benefits to the poor while reducing government spending. But the reduction in government spending is only an illusion. Furthermore, it is not necessarily the poor who would benefit most from selectivity. Unfortunately there is no magic way to improve benefits for the poor without increasing burdens for others. In a model income security system the burden of redistribution would be borne on an ability-to-pay basis.

Bibliography

Balfour, F. and C. Beach (1979) 'Toward the estimation of payroll tax incidence in Canada.' Paper presented to the Conference on Canadian Incomes, Winnipeg, sponsored by the Economic Council of Canada

Barer, M., R. Evans, and G. Stoddart (1979) *Controlling Health Care Costs by Direct Charges to Patients: Snare or Delusion?* (Toronto: Ontario Economic Council)

Barro, R. (1974) 'Are government bonds net wealth?' *Journal of Political Economy* 82, 1095-1117

Beach, Charles (1981) *Distribution of Income and Wealth in Ontario* (Toronto: University of Toronto Press for the Ontario Economic Council)

Beavis, D.A. and V. Kapur (1977) 'An analysis of the take-up rates of the Old Age Security (OAS) and Guaranteed Income Supplement (GIS) programs.' Staff Working Paper 7706 (Ottawa: Health and Welfare Canada, Policy Research and Long Range Planning (Welfare))

Bergeron, M. (1979) *Social Spending in Canada: Trends and Options* (Ottawa: Canadian Council on Social Development)

Betson, D., D. Greenberg, and R. Kasten (1981) 'Simulation analysis of the economic efficiency and distributional effects of alternative program structures: the negative income tax versus the credit income tax.' In J. Garfinkel (1981a)

Beveridge, Sir W. (1942) *Report on Social Insurance and Allied Services* (London: HMSO)

Billet, C., D. Komus, D. Hum, A. Basilevsky, and R. Sproule (1979) 'Issues in the administration of Mincome Manitoba: three preliminary assessments.' Technical Report No. 11 (Winnipeg: Mincome)

Bird, R. (1976) *Charging for Public Services* (Toronto: Canadian Tax Foundation)

Bird, R. and N.E. Slack (1978) *Residential Property Tax Relief in Ontario* (Toronto: University of Toronto Press for the Ontario Economic Council)

Break, George F. (1974) 'The incidence and economic effects of taxation.' Pp. 119–237 in Alan S. Blinder, Robert M. Solow, George F. Break, Peter O. Steiner, and Dick Netzer, *The Economics of Public Finance* (Washington DC: Brookings Institution)

Bryden, K. (1974) *Old Age Pensions and Policy-Making in Canada* (Montreal: McGill-Queen's University Press)

Canada (1970) *Income Security for Canadians* (Ottawa: Health and Welfare)

Canada (1973) *Working Paper on Social Security in Canada* (Ottawa: Health and Welfare)

Canada (1975) *Background Paper on Income Support and Supplementation* (Ottawa: Federal-Provincial Social Security Review)

Canada (1978) 'Integration of social program payments into the income tax system' (Ottawa: Department of Finance)

Canada (1979) *Government of Canada Tax Expenditure Account* (Ottawa: Department of Finance)

Canadian Council on Social Development (1979) 'The future of social security in Canada' (Ottawa: CCSD)

Chan, E. and D. Hum (1980) 'Do minorities participate in Canada's Old Age Security programs? A case study of the Chinese.' *Canadian Public Policy* 6, 646–7

Cloutier, J.E. (1978) 'The distribution of benefits and costs of social security in Canada, 1971–75.' Discussion Paper No. 108. (Ottawa: Economic Council of Canada)

Cloutier, J. and A. Smith (1980) 'The evaluation of an alternative unemployment insurance plan.' Discussion Paper No. 159. (Ottawa: Economic Council of Canada)

Crest, D., C. Billett, D. Hum, D. Komus, and A. Quarry (1979) 'The administration of the payments system of Mincome Manitoba' Technical Report No. 4 (Winnipeg: Mincome)

Crispo, J. (1979) *Mandate for Canada* (Don Mills: General Publishing)

Economic Council of Canada (1978) *A Time for Reason* (Ottawa)

– (1979) *One in Three: Pensions for Canadians to 2030* (Ottawa)

Evans, R. and M. Williamson (1978) *Extending Canadian Health Insurance: Options for Pharmacare and Denticare* (Toronto: University of Toronto Press for the Ontario Economic Council)

Fallis, George (1980) *Housing Programs and Income Distribution in Ontario* (Toronto: University of Toronto Press for the Ontario Economic Council)

Feldstein, M. (1974) 'Social security, induced retirement and aggregate capital accumulation.' *Journal of Political Economy* 82, 905–26

Friedman, M. (1962) *Capitalism and Freedom* (Chicago: University of Chicago Press)

Garfinkel, I., ed., (1981a) *Universal versus Income-Tested Transfer Programs*

– (New York: Academic Press) (1981b) 'Overview.' In I. Garfinkel (1981a).

Gillespie, W.I. (1976) 'On the redistribution of income in Canada.' *Canadian Tax Journal* 34, 417–50

Gillespie, W.I. (1978) *In Search of Robin Hood: The Effect of Federal Budgetary Policies During the 1970's on the Distribution of Income in Canada* (Montreal: C.D. Howe Research Institute)

Golladay, F. and R. Haveman (1977) *The Economic Impacts of Tax–transfer Policy* (New York: Academic Press)

Hum, D. (1980) 'Negative income tax experiments: a descriptive survey with special reference to work incentives.' Pp. 127–47 in *Reflections on Canadian Incomes* (Ottawa: Economic Council of Canada)

– (1981) 'Unemployment insurance and work effort: issues, evidence, and policy directions.' (Toronto: Ontario Economic Council)

Hum, D., D. Crest, and D. Komus (1979) 'The design of the payments system of Mincome Manitoba.' (Winnipeg: Mincome Technical Report No. 3

Interprovincial Task Force on Social Security (1980) *The Income Security System in Canada*. Report to the Interprovincial Conference of Ministers Responsible for Social Services (Ottawa: Canadian Intergovernmental Conference Secretariat)

Jump, G.V. and S.A. Rea (1975) 'The impact of the 1971 Unemployment Insurance Act on work incentives and the aggregate labour market.' Report submitted to the Unemployment Insurance Commission (Institute for the Quantitative Analysis of Social and Economic Policy, University of Toronto)

Kapsalis C. (1980) 'In defence of Family Allowances.' *Canadian Public Policy* 6, 107–9

Keeley, M., O.K. Robins, R.G. Spiegelman, and R.W. Wost (1978) 'The labor-supply effects and costs of alternative NIT.' *Journal of Human Resources* 13, 3–36

Kesselman, J.R. (1971) 'Conditional subsidies in income maintenance.' Western Economic Journal 9, 1–20

– (1979) 'Credits, exemptions and demogrants in Canadian tax transfer policy.' *Canadian Tax Journal* 27, 653–88

- (1981a) 'Pitfalls of selectivity in income security programs.' *Canadian Taxation* 2
Kesselman, J.R. (1981b) 'Taxpayer behavior and the design of a credit income tax.' In I. Garfinkel (1981a)
Kesselman, J.R. and I. Garfinkel (1978) 'Professor Friedman, meet Lady Rhys-Williams: NIT vs CIT.' *Journal of Public Economics* 10, 179–216
Lampman, Robert J. (1978) 'Labor supply and social welfare benefits in the United States.' Paper prepared for National Commission on Employment and Unemployment Statistics (Madison, Wisc.: Institute for Research on Poverty)
Masters, Stanley and Irwin Garfinkel (1977) *Estimating the Labor Supply Effects of Income-Maintenance Alternatives* (New York: Academic Press)
Mendelson, M. (1979) *The Administrative Cost of Income Security Programs: Ontario and Canada* (Toronto: Ontario Economic Council)
- (1980) 'The selectivity mistake.' *Canadian Taxation* 2, 167–9
Morgan, Alison (1980) 'The impact of transfers on the distribution of income in Quebec: elements of analysis applied to certain programmes.' Pp. 149–73 in *Reflections on Canadian Incomes* (Ottawa: Economic Council of Canada)
Musgrave, Richard A. (1959) *The Theory of Public Finance* (New York: McGraw-Hill)
- (1968) 'The role of social insurance in an overall program for social welfare.' Pp. 23–47 in *The Princeton Symposium on the American System of Social Insurance* (New York: McGraw-Hill)
Musgrave, R. and P. Musgrave (1976) *Public Finance in Theory and Practice*. 2nd edition (New York: McGraw-Hill)
Ontario (1979) 'Public pensions and personal savings: Canadian evidence in the extended life cycle model.' Mimeo. (Ministry of Treasury, Economics and Intergovernmental Affairs)
Ontario Economic Council (1979) *Issues and Alternatives: Update 1979* (Toronto)
Osberg, Lars (1979) 'Unemployment insurance in Canada: a review of the recent amendments.' *Canadian Public Policy* 2, 223–35
Pesando, J. and S. Rea, jr (1977) *Public and Private Pensions in Canada: an Economic Analysis* (Toronto: University of Toronto Press for the Ontario Economic Council)
Quebec (1979) *Quebec–Canada: A New Deal* (Quebec: Éditeur officiel du Québec)
- (1971) *Report of the Commission of Inquiry on Health and Social Welfare*, vol. 5: Income Security (Quebec: Éditeur officiel du Québec)

Rea, Samuel A., jr (1974) 'Incentive effects of alternative NIT plans.' *Journal of Public Economics* 3, 237–49

– (1977) 'Unemployment insurance and labour supply: a simulation of the 1971 Unemployment Insurance Act.' *Canadian Journal of Economics* 10, 263–78

– (1981) 'Redistribution effects of Canada's public pension programs' (Ottawa: Economic Council of Canada)

– (forthcoming) *Disability Insurance and Public Policy* (Toronto: University of Toronto Press for the Ontario Economic Council)

Reuber, G. (1978) 'The impact of government policies on the distribution of income in Canada: a review' *Canadian Public Policy* 4, 505–29

Sabourin, D. and D. Hum (1979) 'An analysis of non-response to the Manitoba basic annual income experiment.' Technical Report No. 7 (Winnipeg: Mincome)

Saskatchewan (1976) 'Income support and supplementation: the Saskatchewan experience with the Family Income Plan and the Saskatchewan Assistance Plan.' Mimeo. (Regina: Department of Social Services)

Simeon, R. (1972) *Federal–Provincial Diplomacy* (Toronto: University of Toronto Press)

Simon, W.E. (1979) *A Time for Truth* (Toronto: Totem Books)

Smiley, D. (1972) *Canada in Question: Federalism in the Seventies* (Toronto: McGraw-Hill)

Smith, A., D. Henderson, and J. Cloutier (1979) 'Poverty and government income support in Canada, 1971–1975: characteristics of the low income population.' Discussion Paper No. 130 (Ottawa: Economic Council of Canada)

Statistics Canada (1975) *Income Distribution by Size in Canada*. Cat. 13–207 (Ottawa)

– (1976) *Social Security, National Programs*. Cat. 86–201 (Ottawa)

– (annual) *Consolidated Government Finance: Fiscal Year Ended Nearest to December 31*. Cat. 68–202 (Ottawa)

– (annual) *Government Finance in Accordance with the System of National Accounts*. Cat. 68–001 (Ottawa)

– (annual) *Systems of National Accounts: National Income and Expenditure Accounts*. Cat. 13–201 (Ottawa)

Swan, N., P. MacRae, and C. Steinberg (1976) *Income Maintenance Programs: Their Effect on Labour Supply and Aggregate Demand in the Maritimes* (Ottawa: Economic Council of Canada)

Thurow, L.C. (1975) 'The economics of public finance.' *National Tax Journal* 28, 185–94

Titmuss, R.M. (1968) *Commitment to Welfare* (London: George Allen and Unwin)

Trudeau, P. (1970) *Income Security and Social Services* (Ottawa: Information Canada)

Van Loon, R. (1979) 'Reforming welfare in Canada.' *Public Policy* 27, 469–504

Walker, Michael (1980) 'Measuring and coping with a progressive tax system or robin hoodery – a Canadian tradition past its prime.' *Canadian Taxation* 2, 8–15

Williamson, John B. (1974) 'The stigma of public dependency: a comparison of alternative forms of public aid to the poor.' *Social Problems* 22, 213–28

Wolfson, Michael (1980a) 'The lifetime impact of the retirement income system: a quantitative analysis.' Pp. 51–66 in *Reflections on Canadian Incomes* (Ottawa: Economic Council of Canada)

– (1980b) 'Tax incidence in Canada: Robin Hood on thin ice.' *Canadian Taxation* 2, 123–8